Nomadic Nature

A Comprehensive Guide to RV Camping in National Treasures

James Patterson

Table of Contents

INTRODUCTION

The siren songs of the RV lifestyle are the call of the open road, the aroma of pine-scented forests, and the sound of a bubbling brook. They entice travelers to embark on a voyage of unmatched freedom and discovery. With "Nomadic Nature: A Comprehensive Guide to RV Camping in National Treasures," we invite you to enter a world where your backyard is a kaleidoscope of natural wonders and your home is mobile.

For outdoor enthusiasts, national parks have always had a special place in their hearts because of their breathtaking landscapes and varied ecosystems. However, the union of the recreational vehicle (RV) and the national park results in an unmatched experience, where the voyage itself enriches the final destination. This all-inclusive guide is your ticket to discovering the allure of motorhome camping in some of the country's most famous and pristine sites. Whether you're an experienced RV traveler looking for fresh perspectives or a beginner planning your first trip, "Nomadic Nature" is a must-have companion.

We'll give you the information and resources you need in the following pages so you can plan amazing trips through national parks, experience the wonders of our natural treasures, and live the RV lifestyle. Put on your seatbelts, get ready to embrace the spirit of nomadism, and let "Nomadic Nature" lead you into an exciting and never-ending world of discovery.

CHAPTER I

The RV Lifestyle

Benefits of RV camping

Recreational vehicle camping, or RV camping, is a growingly popular method of experiencing the freedom of the open road and the great outdoors. RV enthusiasts attract people from diverse backgrounds to their way of life because this mode of transportation provides distinct benefits. We will discuss the many advantages of RV camping in this section, including its unmatched sense of community and connection to nature, as well as its comfort and convenience.

The convenience that comes with RV camping is one of its biggest advantages. RVs have contemporary conveniences, unlike traditional camping, which requires you to set up a tent, struggle with cooking over a campfire, and deal with the weather. You have a fully equipped kitchen, a cozy bed, and even a bathroom with electricity and running water. This convenience makes camping easier and frees up more time for you to enjoy the outdoors and less time doing chores.

Furthermore, RV camping offers a degree of comfort that is difficult to find in other outdoor lodging options. You have easy access to climate control, can easily cook meals, and can sleep in your own bed. This comfort factor is particularly appealing to older people or families with small children who might find traditional camping less accessible.

Beyond comfort and convenience, RV camping provides a special chance to get in touch with the natural world. Many RV parks are tucked away in beautiful natural settings, giving visitors easy access to peaceful scenery, hiking trails, and wildlife viewing opportunities. Awakening to the sound of singing birds and the sight of a spotless lake directly outside your recreational vehicle provides a revitalizing experience that uplifts and invigorates the spirit.

Additionally, RV camping enables you to appreciate the beauty of various seasons fully. RV campers can plan their travels to coincide with the natural wonders of each season, whether it's taking in the brilliant fall foliage, seeing the return of spring, or exploring a winter wonderland. The ability to chase the changing of the seasons gives RV camping an exciting new dimension.

Traveling in an RV also promotes a feeling of camaraderie among passengers. Numerous campgrounds provide common areas where guests can gather, exchange tales, and establish camaraderie. Everywhere you go, the RVing community creates a warm and inviting atmosphere because of its reputation for camaraderie and willingness to assist other travelers. You're likely to meet people who share your passion for adventure and the great outdoors whether you're traveling alone or in a group.

Additionally, traveling in an RV gives you more freedom and flexibility. RVers are free to alter their plans at any time, visiting new places or extending their stay at a favorite location, unlike guests at hotels or resorts who have set reservations. This adaptability enables visitors to adjust to shifting weather patterns, unforeseen discoveries, or the simple desire to spend a little more time in an enthralling place.

RV camping is a travel option that encourages self-sufficiency. RVers develop effective resource management skills, from meal preparation and route planning to water and electricity conservation. Being independent makes one feel accomplished and increases awareness of the environment and the need for resource conservation.

In conclusion, RV camping is a desirable choice for individuals looking for comfort, adventure, and a closer relationship with the natural world because it provides a host of advantages. There are many compelling reasons why RV camping is becoming increasingly popular, including the comfort and convenience of RVs, the chance to immerse oneself in natural beauty, the sense of community among fellow campers, the flexibility of travel plans, and the development of self-sufficiency skills. The advantages of RV camping are certain to enhance your travel experiences and leave enduring memories of the great outdoors, regardless of whether you are an experienced traveler or are thinking about taking your first trip.

Types of RVs and their advantages

Recreational vehicles, or RVs, are made to fit various tastes and lifestyles. They are available in a wide range of sizes and shapes. Travelers can experience comfort and convenience as they explore the world in these adaptable vehicles that serve as a home away from home. In this section, we will examine the various types of RVs and their distinctive benefits to assist aspiring RV enthusiasts in making an informed decision based on their needs and preferences.

The Class A motorhome is one of the most popular varieties of RVs. These are known as "home-away-from-home" RVs because of their opulent and roomy interiors. Class A motorhomes often include all the conveniences one would find in a regular home, such as complete kitchens, bathrooms, entertainment systems, and cozy sleeping quarters. They are perfect for long-term travel or full-time living on the road because of their large size, which provides ample living space and storage. Class A motorhomes have the advantage of offering unparalleled comfort, which makes them appropriate for vacationers who value space and luxury.

Conversely, class B motorhomes are smaller and easier to maneuver. These RVs, also known as camper vans, are easy to drive and park because they are constructed on van chassis. Although Class B motorhomes are less spacious than Class A models, they are significantly more fuel-efficient and provide the advantages of off-grid and urban camping. Their smaller size enables access to more remote and picturesque locations, making them ideal for couples or single travelers seeking a flexible and agile RV experience.

Mini-motorhomes, or class C motorhomes, are a compromise between class A and class B. They have an attached cab-over bunk that adds more sleeping space and are constructed on a truck or van chassis. The finest of both worlds are provided by class C motorhomes, which have cozy living areas and easy access to various campgrounds. They are an excellent option for families because of their adaptability because they can usually accommodate several people for sleeping.

Travel trailers are a compelling alternative for individuals who wish to have the freedom of RV travel without the commitment of owning a large motorhome. These recreational vehicles range in size and style from compact teardrop trailers to spacious fifth-wheel trailers. Travel trailers allow for greater vehicle choice when it comes to towing vehicles because they are pulled by a different vehicle, like a truck or SUV. They are perfect for campers who don't want to drive a big motorhome or who already have a suitable towing vehicle. Travel trailers can be easily detachable from the towing vehicle, which lets campers use their car for errands or day trips without having to load up the entire RV.

A subclass of travel trailers called fifth-wheel trailers is distinguished by its special hitching mechanism. Using a specialized fifth-wheel hitch, they are attached to a pickup truck's bed, distributing weight more evenly and frequently enabling larger living spaces. These trailers are a popular option for long-term travel or permanent residence because of their roomy interiors and many luxurious amenities. Fifth-wheel trailers have the benefit of stability and ease of towing because of the hitching system's increased control and maneuverability.

Toy haulers are a different kind of RV that is growing in popularity. Adventurers who wish to travel with recreational vehicles like motorcycles, ATVs, or kayaks can choose from these RVs. These vehicles can be transported and stored in the garage area found at the back of toy haulers. The garage can be used as a flexible living or sleeping space when the toys are taken out. Toy haulers, which appeal to thrill-seekers and outdoor enthusiasts, have the benefit of combining outdoor adventure with RV comfort.

Lastly, pop-up campers are a lightweight and reasonably priced choice for those wishing to get started in RVing. These collapsible trailers are perfect for first-time campers or those seeking a more straightforward camping experience because they are simple to tow and set up. Pop-up campers allow campers to enjoy the great outdoors without sacrificing too many comforts, even though they have fewer amenities than larger RVs. They still offer a comfortable sleeping area and basic kitchen facilities.

In conclusion, the world of recreational vehicles is broad and offers a variety of options to suit different tastes and lifestyles. There is an RV type to suit your needs, regardless of your priorities—space, mobility, fuel economy, or the capacity to transport outdoor toys. Knowing the benefits of each type of RV will enable you to choose wisely and confidently set out on your travels with the knowledge that you have chosen the ideal mobile home.

Budget considerations

Taking a trip with an RV and exploring the great outdoors while enjoying the conveniences of home on wheels is an exciting prospect. To guarantee a smooth and enjoyable trip, it is imperative to consider financial considerations before embarking on the journey. In this section, we will examine the numerous financial factors that prospective RV campers need to be aware of, covering everything from the initial RV purchase to recurring costs and money-saving techniques.

The initial cost of purchasing an RV is one of the most important financial factors to consider when going RV camping. RVs have many different styles and sizes, each with a price tag. Smaller Class B motorhomes and travel trailers provide more affordable options, while Class A motorhomes, which are prized for their roominess and luxury, are typically the most costly. Your travel preferences and financial constraints should be considered when selecting an RV. Used RVs can save a lot of money but might need more maintenance and repairs. New RVs are more expensive but usually have warranties and the newest features.

It's important to account for the costs of insurance, registration, and taxes in addition to the RV purchase price. RV insurance is crucial to safeguard your investment and offer liability, damage, and accident coverage. State-specific taxes and registration fees may increase the initial cost of ownership. Effective management of these costs can be achieved by investigating and contrasting insurance options and comprehending state-specific regulations.

After you purchase your RV, continuing costs become an essential factor to consider. Fuel expenses account for a sizeable portion of the budget for RV camping because these vehicles are typically less fuel-efficient than regular cars. How much fuel you use will depend on your travel style, the weight and size of your RV, and other factors. Consider traveling during off-peak hours, carefully plan your routes, and use fuel-efficient driving techniques to reduce fuel expenses.

Another recurring cost to consider is campground fees. The cost of a campground can vary greatly, ranging from free or inexpensive public campgrounds to upscale private resorts with first-rate amenities. Plan ahead for your campground visits by researching and weighing your desired level of comfort and convenience against your financial constraints. Additionally, some campers look into boondocking or dispersed camping, which can drastically cut costs by enabling free camping on public lands (though without utilities).

The costs of upkeep and repairs are a necessary component of owning an RV. Maintaining the optimal functioning of your RV requires routine maintenance, which includes tire inspections, oil changes, and appliance inspections. Setting aside money for regular maintenance helps avert larger, more expensive repairs in the future. Setting aside money for unforeseen maintenance or emergencies while traveling is also a smart idea. You can feel more at ease and be ready for unforeseen costs if you have a safety net of finances.

Considering that RVers frequently enjoy the convenience of a fully functional kitchen, food and groceries are constant budget concerns. Even though going out to eat occasionally can be fun, cooking in your RV can result in significant cost savings. Plan your meals, buy your groceries at stores that offer discounts, and utilize outdoor grills and campfire cooking to improve your cooking while minimizing expenses.

Entertainment and activities are a crucial component of the budget. Although many outdoor activities are available when RV camping, some may have a cost, such as park entrance fees, guided tours, or equipment rentals. To get the most out of your natural surroundings without going over budget, budget for these activities in advance and think about looking into free or inexpensive alternatives like hiking, bird watching, or stargazing. Adopting cost-saving measures is also a smart idea if you want to maximize your RV camping budget. Planning longer stays in each place can help cut down on the number of times the RV needs to be moved and the fuel expenses that go along with it. In addition, discounts on campgrounds and services can be obtained by signing up for RV clubs and loyalty programs. RVers on a tight budget might also look into workamping, a practice where people trade a part-time job for free or heavily discounted campsite stays.

In conclusion, RV camping gives you the flexibility to experience the comforts of home while exploring the natural beauty of the outdoors. It is imperative to take into account multiple budgetary aspects in order to guarantee a financially viable and pleasurable encounter. A well-thought-out budget plan will enable you to set out on your RV camping adventure with confidence, knowing that you can enjoy the trip without going over budget. It will cover everything from the initial purchase and insurance costs to ongoing expenses and cost-saving techniques.

Preparing for life on the road

The freedom to travel, explore, and experience life on the open road is what makes RV camping so appealing. However, adopting a nomadic lifestyle necessitates thorough planning and thought-out consideration of many factors. This section will review the important actions and things to consider when getting ready for life on the road, such as choosing the best RV, making a route plan, and adopting a minimalist approach.

Choosing the ideal RV for your requirements and tastes is one of the first steps in getting ready for life on the road. RVs are available in various shapes, sizes, and price points, as was covered in a previous section. Your selection should fit your intended level of comfort, travel preferences, and financial constraints. Examine various RV models online, go to dealerships to see them in person, and take into account features like sleeping arrangements, facilities, and storage space. Your RV will eventually become your home, so picking one that fits your lifestyle is important.

Once you've purchased your RV, it's critical to familiarize yourself with its functions and systems. Spend some time learning the safe driving and towing techniques for your recreational vehicle, taking note of its size and handling characteristics. Learn about the HVAC, plumbing, and electrical systems on board. While traveling, troubleshooting common problems can save time and frustration. Many RV manufacturers provide orientation sessions to new owners, and they can be very helpful in building confidence and competence in RV ownership.

One of the most important parts of getting ready for life on the road is planning your route. Although RV travel encourages spontaneity, planning ahead can help you get the most out of your trip. Think about the places you wish to visit, the times of year you want to travel, and the duration of your trip. Keep in mind that some roads may not be suitable for RVs due to their size or weight restrictions. Use RV-friendly GPS or apps to avoid such routes. Examine available campsites and RV parks along your route, paying attention to their costs, amenities, and availability. You can give your journey some structure by making a rough travel schedule, but you can also leave room for flexibility and side trips.

A vital first step in getting ready for life on the road is to downsize and organize your belongings. Living in an RV often requires a minimalist approach due to its limited space. Give your belongings a thorough inspection and rank the necessities first. Things that won't fit in your RV or aren't essential for your trip should be donated, sold, or stored. Adopting a minimalist lifestyle makes the shift easier and frees you up to prioritize experiences over material belongings.

Financial planning is an additional essential component of preparation. Establish your RV living budget, considering costs for food, entertainment, insurance, maintenance, gas, and campground fees. Make an emergency budget to cover unexpected costs and roadside emergencies. Think about automating bill payments, setting up online banking, carrying cash or debit/credit cards for different kinds of transactions, and managing your finances while on the road. You'll be able to travel with peace of mind and confidence if you have a well-thought-out financial plan that covers all the bases.

Safety needs to be your first concern when getting ready for RV life. Ensure your recreational vehicle (RV) has all the necessary safety equipment, such as first aid kits, fire extinguishers, carbon monoxide detectors, and also smoke detectors. Create a safety checklist before leaving and arriving at campgrounds to help you prevent common mishaps and mistakes. Learn about the safety precautions unique to RVs, such as appropriate weight distribution, tire maintenance, and emergency protocols. You may travel worry-free by being aware of safety precautions and exercising caution when taking them.

It's getting more and more crucial to live an eco-friendly and sustainable lifestyle in your recreational vehicle. Adopting eco-friendly habits like water conservation, energy conservation, and Leave No Trace principles can help you lessen your environmental impact. Use solar energy and energy-saving appliances, dispose of waste properly, and donate to organizations and campgrounds that encourage environmentally friendly RVing. You can protect the inherent beauty of the places you visit for future generations by using minimal environmental impact.

Getting ready for life on the road is a complex process that includes selecting the ideal RV, learning how to operate it, organizing your itinerary, embracing minimalism, handling money, putting safety first, and implementing eco-friendly habits. Even though the adjustment might take some time and work, RV living's benefits—freedom, adventure, and a closer bond with the natural world—make the preparation worthwhile. As you set out on your adventure, remember that living on the road is a singular and fulfilling experience that lets you experience the freedom of seeing the world as you see fit and the exhilaration of being on the open road.

CHAPTER II

Planning Your National Park Adventure

Selecting the right national parks

The United States boasts diverse national parks, each with unique natural wonders, ecosystems, and cultural heritage. For RV enthusiasts and nature lovers, choosing the right national parks to visit can be both exhilarating and challenging. This section will explore the factors to take into account when selecting the right national parks for your RV camping adventure, emphasizing the importance of aligning your interests, preferences, and travel goals with the parks you choose to explore.

One of the first considerations when selecting national parks is your personal interests and the activities you enjoy. National parks offer various outdoor experiences, from hiking and wildlife watching to photography and stargazing. If you're passionate about hiking, you might gravitate toward parks renowned for their extensive trail systems, such as Yosemite National Park in California or Acadia National Park in Maine. On the other hand, if you're an avid birdwatcher, places like Florida's Everglades National Park or Tennessee's Great Smoky Mountains National Park provide excellent opportunities to see a variety of birds. By aligning your interests with the activities and ecosystems found in specific parks, you can ensure a more fulfilling and rewarding experience.

The time of year you plan to visit also plays a significant role in park selection. Different seasons bring varying weather conditions, wildlife activity, and natural beauty to national parks. For instance, New England parks such as Virginia's Shenandoah National Park or Great Smoky Mountains provide breathtaking autumnal views if you're eager to see the colorful fall foliage. On the other hand, if you prefer mild weather for outdoor activities, consider visiting parks in the spring or fall when temperatures are more comfortable. Be sure to research the best times to visit each park to make the most of your RV camping adventure.

Access and travel logistics are essential factors when choosing national parks. RV camping accessibility can vary greatly from park to park, with some parks offering a range of RV-friendly campgrounds while others may have size restrictions or limited amenities. Confirming that your chosen parks can accommodate your RV size and provide the necessary hookups or facilities is crucial. Additionally, consider the proximity of the parks to one another if you plan to visit multiple destinations during your journey. Efficient route planning can assist you in optimizing your travel time and minimize driving distances between parks.

The cultural and historical importance of national parks also influences the selection process. Some parks, like Yellowstone National Park in Wyoming, Montana, and Idaho, or Mesa Verde National Park in Colorado, offer a glimpse into indigenous peoples' and early settlers' rich cultural heritage, with well-preserved archaeological sites and historic structures. These parks provide opportunities to connect with the past and gain a more profound appreciation for the region's history. If cultural exploration is a priority, be sure to include parks with significant historical value in your itinerary.

A crucial aspect of selecting national parks for RV camping is understanding their popularity and the potential for crowds. Iconic parks like Grand Canyon National Park in

Arizona or Zion National Park in Utah attract millions of visitors each year, especially during peak seasons. While these parks offer breathtaking landscapes and experiences, they may require advanced planning, early reservations, and a willingness to explore less-visited areas within the parks. If you prefer a quieter and more serene RV camping experience, consider exploring lesser- known or remote national parks where you can immerse yourself in nature without the crowds.

Finally, take into account the duration of your RV camping adventure. If you have limited time, focusing on parks within a specific region can help you make the most of your journey without spending excessive time on the road. Conversely, if you have an extended timeframe, you may have the opportunity to embark on a cross-country adventure, visiting a diverse range of national parks and experiencing the vastness and beauty of the American landscape.

In conclusion, selecting the right national parks for your RV camping adventure involves thoughtful consideration of your interests, the season of your visit, access and logistics, cultural and historical significance, crowd preferences, and the journey duration. National parks provide a treasure trove of natural wonders and outdoor experiences, each with its unique charm and appeal. By aligning your preferences and goals with the parks you choose to explore, you can embark on an RV camping adventure that is both fulfilling and unforgettable, connecting with the natural world and creating cherished memories along the way.

Seasonal considerations

The changing seasons bring RV camping enthusiasts a kaleidoscope of experiences and challenges. Whether you're planning a summer road trip, a winter escape, or a journey during the shoulder seasons, understanding the unique aspects of each season is essential for a successful and enjoyable RV camping adventure. In this section, we will explore the seasonal considerations that RV campers should consider, from weather and climate to campground availability and activity opportunities.

Summer is the most common season for RV camping, and for good reason. Warm weather, longer daylight hours, and lush landscapes make it an ideal time to explore national parks and natural wonders. However, the popularity of summer camping also means crowded campgrounds and the need for advanced reservations in many sought-after locations. High temperatures can also be challenging, especially in regions with scorching summer heat. It's essential to have proper insulation and cooling systems in your RV to stay comfortable. Be prepared for occasional afternoon thunderstorms and bugs, and consider planning outdoor activities for the cooler mornings and evenings. Summer offers a vibrant and bustling RV camping experience, perfect for families and outdoor enthusiasts.

With its crisp air and vibrant foliage, fall is a favorite season for many RV campers. National parks in New England, such as Acadia and the White Mountains, offer breathtaking displays of autumn colors. Parks like Yosemite and the Rocky Mountains are enchanting in the western United States. The cooler temperatures of fall make outdoor activities like hiking and biking more enjoyable, and the smaller crowds provide a more tranquil camping experience. However, advanced planning is still advisable, as fall foliage attracts visitors from far and wide. Be prepared for varying weather conditions, as fall can bring chilly nights and occasional rain. Fall offers a serene and picturesque RV camping experience, focusing on natural beauty and outdoor exploration.
Winter RV camping is an adventure and a unique experience for those seeking solitude. While many RVers

choose to winterize their vehicles and store them for the season, some embrace the cold and explore winter wonderlands. Popular destinations for winter RV camping include the deserts of the American Southwest, where mild daytime temperatures contrast with chilly nights. Snowbird destinations in Florida and Arizona provide a warm respite from the northern cold. To enjoy winter RV camping, it's crucial to have adequate insulation, a reliable heating system, and knowledge of cold-weather camping techniques. Be prepared for shorter daylight hours and the need to conserve water and manage waste in freezing temperatures. Winter camping offers a peaceful, off-the-beaten-path experience, perfect for those seeking tranquility and a connection with the winter landscape.

Spring marks the awakening of nature, with wildflowers blooming and wildlife becoming active once more. Many RV campers flock to national parks in the spring to witness this rejuvenation. Parks like Great Smoky Mountains, Shenandoah, and Joshua Tree offer splendid springtime displays. Spring temperatures are generally mild and pleasant, making it an ideal time for outdoor activities. However, it's essential to be aware of potential weather fluctuations and the possibility of rain. Spring camping can be a bit unpredictable, but the rewards include lush landscapes, vibrant colors, and the opportunity to observe wildlife during the breeding season. Spring offers a rejuvenating and nature-focused RV camping experience, perfect for those who relish the beauty of renewal.

Shoulder seasons, which fall between the peak seasons of summer and fall or winter and spring, offer a unique blend of advantages. Campgrounds are less crowded, allowing for greater flexibility and spontaneity in travel plans. Mild temperatures make outdoor activities comfortable, and the landscapes may still showcase some of the beauty of the previous season. However, shoulder seasons can be transitional, with changing weather patterns and potential challenges like snowmelt or early frosts. RV campers should be prepared for variable conditions and closely monitor weather forecasts. Shoulder seasons provide a balanced and less-crowded RV camping experience, ideal for those seeking a mix of solitude and outdoor adventure.

In conclusion, understanding seasonal considerations is paramount for a successful and enjoyable RV camping adventure. Each season offers unique charm and challenges, from crowded summer campgrounds to chilly winter nights and the unpredictable spring and fall weather. By aligning your preferences, tolerance for crowds, and weather-related plans with the season of your choice, you can make the most of your RV camping journey and create lasting memories in America's national treasures. Whether you seek vibrant landscapes, tranquil solitude, or a blend of experiences, there's a perfect season for your RV adventure.

Reservations and permits

RV camping in national parks is a dream come true for many outdoor enthusiasts. The allure of waking up to stunning natural vistas, exploring pristine wilderness, and immersing oneself in the beauty of the great outdoors is undeniably enticing. However, navigating the world of reservations and permits is essential to turn this dream into a reality. In this section, we will delve into the intricacies of reservations and permits when planning an RV camping adventure in national parks, highlighting the importance of advanced planning, the diversity of reservation systems, and the need to respect permit requirements.

Advanced planning is a cornerstone of successful RV camping in national parks, and this often begins with securing reservations. As the popularity of national parks continues to rise, especially during peak seasons, securing a campsite can be a competitive endeavor. Most national parks offer online reservation systems, which allow campers to book their campsites months in advance. Research and familiarize yourself with the reservation windows for your desired parks, as they can vary widely. For instance, some campgrounds open reservations six months ahead, while others may open them a year in advance. Knowing the opening dates and times for reservations is crucial to secure your preferred camping dates.

Additionally, it's essential to be aware of the diversity of reservation systems used in national parks. While the National Park Service (NPS) manages many parks, others are under the jurisdiction of state or local authorities. Each entity may have its reservation system, and the rules and procedures can differ significantly. For instance, some parks utilize a lottery system for highly sought-after campgrounds, while others offer first-come, first-served sites. Understanding the specific reservation policies and procedures for each park you plan to visit is essential to avoid disappointment and frustration.

Permits are another critical aspect of RV camping in national parks, especially when engaging in specific activities or visiting more remote or protected areas. Permits may be required for activities such as backcountry camping, hiking, boating, fishing, or photography. Permits are meant to manage visitor use, protect sensitive environments, and ensure a safe and enjoyable experience for all. Before embarking on activities requiring permits, thoroughly research the park's regulations and requirements. Familiarize yourself with the application process, fees, and any seasonal restrictions.

When applying for permits, it's crucial to do so well in advance, as some permits are limited and may be subject to high demand. For example, obtaining a permit to hike the iconic Narrows trail in Zion National Park or to raft the Grand Canyon can be highly competitive, with applicants often vying for limited slots. Early planning and persistence are key to securing these coveted permits.

Respect for permit requirements is a fundamental principle of responsible RV camping in national parks. Failure to comply with permit regulations puts the natural environment at risk and can result in fines and penalties. Follow the guidelines provided by park authorities, such as campfire restrictions, waste disposal procedures, and wildlife viewing guidelines. Additionally, be aware of permit terms and conditions, such as entry and exit dates, group size limits, and camping zones. Adhering to these regulations ensures you enjoy your RV camping adventure while preserving the park's ecological integrity and cultural heritage.

In some cases, permits may be required for specific activities and entrance to the park itself. The National Park Service operates a fee system, where park entrance fees contribute to the maintenance and preservation of the parks. However, these fees have several exceptions, including free admission days and passes for senior citizens, active-duty military personnel, and fourth-grade students. Consider whether an annual pass, such as the America the Beautiful Pass, which gives access to all federal lands and waters, is a cost-effective option for your RV camping adventures. These passes can offer substantial savings for frequent park visitors.

In conclusion, reservations and permits are integral components of planning a successful RV camping adventure in national parks. Advanced planning, a thorough understanding of reservation systems, and compliance with permit requirements are essential to securing your desired camping dates, accessing specific activities, and respecting the natural and cultural resources of the parks. While the process may seem complex at times, the rewards of RV camping in national parks—unforgettable experiences, stunning landscapes, and a deeper connection with nature—are well worth the effort and diligence required to navigate the world of reservations and permits. By respecting park regulations and being prepared, you can embark on a memorable and responsible RV camping journey in America's national treasures.

Trip duration and itinerary planning

When embarking on an RV camping adventure, determining the trip duration and crafting a well-thought-out itinerary are essential steps that can significantly influence the overall experience. Whether you're planning a weekend getaway, an extended road trip, or a full-time RV lifestyle, careful consideration of trip duration and itinerary planning can make the distinction between a memorable journey and a stressful endeavor. This section will explore the factors to take into account when making a decision on the duration of your RV trip and offer tips for crafting a well-balanced and enjoyable itinerary.

The duration of your RV trip is a fundamental decision that sets the tone for your adventure. It can range from a quick weekend escape to a multi-month exploration of diverse destinations. The first step in determining trip duration is to assess your available time and resources. Consider factors such as work commitments, family obligations, and personal preferences. Some RV enthusiasts may have the flexibility to embark on extended journeys, while others may need to plan shorter getaways that align with their schedules. Understanding your constraints and priorities will help you establish a realistic trip duration.

Once you know your available time, you can begin crafting your itinerary. Effective itinerary planning is a balancing act, as it involves maximizing your travel experiences while allowing for relaxation and spontaneity. The key is to balance exploration and leisure, ensuring you make the most of your RV adventure without feeling rushed or overwhelmed.

Begin by choosing your destinations. Consider the places you've always wanted to visit and the activities you want to experience. National parks, scenic byways, historic sites, and vibrant cities are all potential stops along your journey. Research each destination to understand its unique attractions, seasonal considerations, and any reservations or permits required. Take into account the distances between destinations, as well as driving times, to create a feasible and enjoyable route.

It's essential to be realistic about travel distances when planning your itinerary. RV travel typically involves slower speeds and more frequent stops, so accounting for travel time is crucial. While it may be tempting to cover as much ground as possible, rushing from one destination to another can lead to fatigue and missed opportunities for exploration. Plan your driving days with breaks to rest, refuel, and enjoy roadside attractions.

Consider the pace of your journey. Are you the type of traveler who prefers to stay in one place for an extended period, allowing for in-depth exploration, or do you enjoy a faster pace, with a new destination every few days? There's no one-size-fits-all answer, as the ideal pace varies from person to person. However, a good rule of thumb is to balance longer stays with shorter stops. Extended stays in specific locations provide the opportunity to immerse yourself in the culture, activities, and natural beauty of the area, while shorter stops can add variety and spontaneity to your adventure.

Flexibility is a hallmark of RV travel, and your itinerary should allow for unexpected discoveries and detours. While planning is essential, leaving room for serendipitous encounters and last-minute changes can enhance your adventure. Leave open slots in your schedule for exploring hidden gems, following recommendations from fellow travelers, or extending your stay in a particularly captivating location.

As you craft your itinerary, it's essential to prioritize rest and downtime. RV travel can be physically demanding, from driving long distances to setting up and breaking down camp. Adequate rest ensures that you stay alert and energized throughout your journey. Consider incorporating rest days into your itinerary, where you can relax at your campsite, enjoy leisurely activities, or simply unwind. These moments of respite will enhance your overall enjoyment and prevent burnout.

An integral part of itinerary planning is budgeting. Understanding the financial components of your trip is essential for a stress-free experience. Calculate the costs of RV campgrounds, fuel, food, activities, and any entrance fees or permits. Be realistic about your budget and set aside contingency funds for unexpected expenses. Consider meal planning and grocery shopping to manage food expenses and avoid dining out for every meal.

In conclusion, determining the duration of your RV trip and crafting a well-balanced itinerary are crucial steps in ensuring a memorable and enjoyable adventure. Assess your available time and resources, choose your destinations wisely, and plan a pace that aligns with your preferences and energy levels. Factor in rest days and leave room for spontaneity and exploration. Budgeting and financial planning are also essential to avoid financial stress during your journey. Ultimately, a well-planned itinerary sets the stage for an RV adventure filled with discovery, relaxation, and unforgettable experiences, allowing you to savor the beauty of the open road and the wonders of your chosen destinations.

CHAPTER III

RV Essentials

Choosing the right RV for your trip

Starting an RV adventure is a thrilling idea because it gives you the flexibility to travel the country while still enjoying home comforts. But choosing the ideal RV for your journey is an important choice that will have a big impact on how much fun you have traveling. RVs are available in a variety of sizes, shapes, and configurations to suit a range of tastes and modes of transportation. This section will go over the important factors to consider when selecting the ideal RV for your trip, from knowing what kinds of RVs are available to assessing your needs and priorities.

One of the primary factors to consider is the type of RV that best suits your needs. RVs can be broadly categorized into several types, each with its advantages and limitations. Class A motorhomes are often called "home-away-from-home" RVs due to their spacious and luxurious interiors. They typically come equipped with all the amenities one would find in a traditional home, including full kitchens, bathrooms, entertainment systems, and comfortable sleeping areas. Their large size allows for generous living space and storage, making them ideal for long-term travel or full-time living on the road. Class A motorhomes are suitable for travelers who prioritize luxury, space, and a wide range of amenities.

Class B motorhomes, or camper vans, offer a more compact and maneuverable option. These RVs are built on van chassis and are easy to drive and park. While they sacrifice some of the spaciousness of Class A motorhomes, Class B vehicles are much more fuel- efficient and offer the convenience of urban and off-grid camping. They are ideal for couples or even solo travelers seeking an elegant and versatile RV experience. Class B motorhomes provide the essentials for a comfortable journey without the excess space.

Class C motorhomes, sometimes called mini-motorhomes, balance Class A and Class B. They have an attached cab-over bunk that adds more sleeping space, and they are constructed on a truck or van chassis. The finest of both worlds are provided by class C motorhomes, which have cozy living areas and easy access to a variety of campgrounds. Their versatility makes them an excellent choice for families, as they typically offer sleeping accommodations for multiple people.

For those who want the freedom of RV travel without the commitment of owning a large motorhome, travel trailers offer a compelling option. These RVs come in various sizes and configurations, from small teardrop trailers to large fifth-wheel trailers. Travel trailers are towed by a different vehicle, like a truck or SUV, providing more flexibility regarding the choice of towing vehicle. They are ideal for campers with a suitable towing vehicle or prefer not to drive a large motorhome. Travel trailers can be easily detached from the towing vehicle, allowing campers to use their vehicle for day trips or errands without needing to pack up the entire RV.

Fifth-wheel trailers are a subtype of travel trailers known for their unique hitching system. They are linked to the bed of a pickup truck using a specialized fifth-wheel hitch, distributing weight more evenly and often allowing for larger living spaces. These trailers offer spacious interiors and are usually equipped with luxurious amenities, making them a popular choice for extended vacations or full-time living. Fifth-wheel trailers provide the advantage of stability and ease of towing, as the hitching system offers greater control and maneuverability.

Another type of RV gaining popularity is the toy hauler. These RVs are designed for adventurers who want to bring along recreational vehicles like motorcycles, ATVs, or kayaks. Toy haulers typically have a garage area at the rear, which can be used to transport and store these vehicles. The garage space can also serve as a versatile living or sleeping area when the toys are removed. Toy haulers offer the advantage of combining outdoor adventure with RV comfort, catering to thrill-seekers and outdoor enthusiasts.

Lastly, pop-up campers are a lightweight and budget-friendly option for those looking to dip their toes into the world of RVing. These collapsible trailers are easy to tow and set up, making them ideal for novice campers or those who want a simpler camping experience. While they offer fewer amenities than larger RVs, pop-up campers provide a comfortable sleeping space and basic kitchen facilities, allowing campers to enjoy the great outdoors without sacrificing too many comforts.

In addition to considering the type of RV, size and layout are crucial factors to evaluate. RVs come in various lengths and floor plans, and the right choice depends on your travel style and the number of people in your group. Consider the number of sleeping areas, the configuration of the kitchen and dining areas, and the overall layout to ensure it meets your needs. If you plan to spend extended periods in your RV, having a layout that provides comfort and functionality is essential for a pleasant journey.

Another important consideration is your budget. RVs vary widely in price, from affordable options to high-end luxury models. Determine your budget for the RV purchase, considering the initial cost and ongoing expenses such as maintenance, insurance, and campground fees. New RVs come with a higher price tag but often include warranties and the latest amenities, while used RVs can offer significant cost savings but may require more maintenance and repairs. Understanding your budget constraints will help you narrow down your choices and find an RV that aligns with your financial resources.

Additionally, it's essential to consider the practical aspects of RV ownership. Think about where you will store your RV when not in use and whether you have the means to tow or drive it to your desired destinations. Understanding RV ownership's maintenance requirements and potential challenges, such as waste disposal and repairs, is also crucial for a smooth and enjoyable experience.

In conclusion, choosing the right RV for your trip is a significant decision that requires careful consideration of factors such as the type of RV, size and layout, budget, and practical aspects of ownership. Each RV type offers unique advantages, catering to different travel styles and preferences. By assessing your needs and priorities, conducting thorough research, and perhaps even renting or test-driving RVs before purchasing, you can select the perfect home on wheels for your RV adventure. Whether you opt for the spacious luxury of a Class A motorhome, a travel trailer's versatility, or a pop-up camper's simplicity, your RV choice will set the stage for a memorable and comfortable journey on the open road.

Packing checklist

RV camping is a popular outdoor activity that offers the perfect blend of adventure as well as comfort. Whether you're a seasoned RVer or new to the world of recreational vehicle camping, proper preparation is essential to guarantee a successful and enjoyable trip. One of the key aspects of RV camping is having a well-organized packing checklist. This checklist helps you remember all the essential items to bring along, ensuring a comfortable and stress-free experience in the great outdoors.

First and foremost, regarding RV camping, you need to consider your shelter and sleeping arrangements. Ensure you have the RV in good working condition, with all necessary maintenance checks completed. Your RV will serve as your home away from home, so ensure it's equipped with all the amenities you'll need, including a functioning kitchen, bathroom facilities, and comfortable sleeping arrangements. Double-check that you have your RV's registration, insurance, and all the necessary documentation in order.

Kitchen essentials are crucial for a successful RV camping trip. Ensure you have enough pots, pans, and utensils for cooking and eating. Remember to bring your favorite campfire cooking equipment, as many RV campgrounds offer fire pits. If you intend to cook, stock up on fresh ingredients and non-perishable food items. Be mindful of any dietary restrictions or special dietary needs for you and your fellow travelers.

Clean water is essential for drinking and cooking, so ensure your RV's water tank is filled and the plumbing system is in good working order. Additionally, consider bringing a portable water filter or purifier for extra peace of mind, especially if you plan to venture into remote areas where clean water sources may be limited.

Safety should always be a top priority when RV camping. Double-check that your RV has essential safety equipment such as fire extinguishers, smoke detectors, and carbon monoxide detectors. Also, bring a well-stocked first aid kit and familiarize yourself with its contents. It's wise to have a basic tool kit on hand for any unexpected repairs or maintenance that may arise during your trip.

To maximize your enjoyment of the outdoors, you'll want to pack appropriate outdoor gear. This includes camping chairs, a portable grill, and outdoor lighting for evenings around the campfire. Don't forget to bring along recreational equipment such as bicycles, fishing gear, or hiking gear, depending on your interests and the location of your RV campground.

When it comes to clothing, consider your destination's climate and weather conditions. Bring layers of clothes for different temperatures and, just in case, some rain gear. Comfortable footwear suitable for outdoor activities is necessary, whether you plan to hike, bike, or simply explore the surroundings.
Entertainment is another important aspect of RV camping. Bring along books, board games, or any other activities you and your companions enjoy during downtime. Camping is a wonderful chance to disconnect from screens and enjoy quality time together.

In conclusion, a well-prepared packing checklist is essential for a successful RV camping trip. You can confidently embark on your adventure by ensuring you have all the necessary items for shelter, cooking, safety, outdoor activities, and entertainment. Proper planning and organization will make your RV camping experience more enjoyable and help you create lasting memories in the great outdoors. So, start preparing your checklist today and get ready to hit the road for an unforgettable RV camping adventure.

Maintenance and safety tips

Maintaining a safe and functional living space is essential for any homeowner, and the same principle applies to those who own recreational vehicles (RVs). RVs offer a unique way to explore the world while enjoying the comforts of home on the road. However, to ensure a safe and trouble-free journey, it's crucial to prioritize regular maintenance and safety checks. This section will explore the key maintenance and safety tips that every RV owner should follow.

First and foremost, regular maintenance is the cornerstone of RV safety. Before embarking on any trip, it's vital to thoroughly inspect your RV's exterior and interior. Examine the tires for proper inflation, tread wear, and any signs of damage or deterioration. Ensure that all lights, including headlights, taillights, and turn signals, are in working order. Check the brakes, suspension, as well as steering components for any issues, as these are critical for safe driving.

The RV's engine and drivetrain should also be inspected regularly. Change the oil, filters, and other fluids according to the manufacturer's recommendations. Pay attention to the transmission, exhaust system, and cooling system to prevent potential breakdowns on the road. Maintaining the engine ensures that your RV operates smoothly and efficiently, minimizing the danger of unexpected mechanical failures during your journey. In addition to the engine, the RV's living quarters require proper upkeep. Make sure all fixtures, including showerheads, toilets, and faucets, are functioning properly and that the plumbing system is not leaky on a regular basis. Monitor the electrical system, including the wiring and outlets, to avoid potential electrical hazards. Testing the RV's heating and cooling systems to ensure they provide adequate comfort during all seasons is essential.

Fire safety is a paramount concern in any RV. Install smoke and carbon monoxide detectors in critical areas of the RV to provide early warnings in emergencies. Always have a fire extinguisher readily accessible and check its expiration date regularly. Educate yourself and your travel companions on fire safety procedures, including escape routes and how to use the extinguisher.

Properly securing your RV during travel is crucial for safety. Ensure that all items inside the RV are stowed securely to prevent shifting or falling during transit. Lock all cabinets and drawers to prevent contents from spilling out while driving. When parking or setting up camp, use stabilizers and leveling blocks to keep the RV stable and level, reducing the risk of accidents or discomfort while inside.

Another essential aspect of RV safety is understanding weight distribution and load limits. Overloading an RV can lead to reduced stability, increased wear and tear on tires and suspension components, and even accidents. Familiarize yourself with your RV's weight ratings and ensure you evenly distribute your belongings and passengers to stay within those limits.

When it comes to safety on the road, defensive driving is key. RVs are larger and heavier compared to regular vehicles, needing more time and distance to stop. Maintain a secure following distance and be cautious when changing lanes or merging onto highways. Be mindful of low clearances, especially when passing under bridges or entering parking garages.

In conclusion, maintaining and ensuring the safety of your RV is a responsibility that every owner should take seriously. Regular maintenance checks, fire safety precautions, proper weight distribution, and defensive driving are essential elements of RV safety. By following these tips and staying proactive in your RV maintenance routine, you can enjoy your travels with peace of mind, knowing that you've taken the necessary steps to prioritize safety on the road. RV ownership offers a unique opportunity for adventure, and with proper care and attention, it can be a secure and enjoyable way to explore the world.

Setting up your RV campsite

Setting up an RV campsite is an exciting part of the RVing experience, as it allows you to create a temporary home-away-from-home in the great outdoors. Properly preparing your campsite is essential to ensure a comfortable and enjoyable stay. This section will discuss the key steps and considerations for setting up your RV campsite.

The first step in setting up your RV campsite is choosing the right location. Look for a level and well-drained area where you can park your RV. Ensure the site is large enough to accommodate your RV and any additional equipment or amenities you plan to set up, such as awnings, outdoor seating, or a barbecue grill. Consider the distance to amenities like restrooms, water sources, and electrical hookups, if available, as well as the proximity to natural features like lakes, rivers, or hiking trails.

Once you've selected your campsite, it's time to park and level your RV. Use leveling blocks or pads to make sure that your RV is on an even surface, as this provides greater comfort and prevents potential issues with appliances and plumbing. Extend your RV's stabilizing jacks to secure it in place further. If your campsite offers hookups for water, electricity, and sewage, connect your RV to these services as needed.

Setting up the exterior of your campsite involves creating a comfortable and functional outdoor space. Consider deploying an awning or outdoor canopy to provide shade and protection from the elements. Arrange outdoor furniture, such as camping chairs and a table, to create a cozy sitting area. Many RVers also like to set up an outdoor rug to define their campsite and keep dirt and debris at bay.

When it comes to utilities, pay attention to power management. If you are relying on your RV's battery or a generator for electricity, be mindful of your power consumption and conserve energy whenever possible. If you have access to an electrical hookup, use a surge protector to safeguard your RV's electrical system from voltage spikes.

Water management is equally important. Ensure your RV's fresh water tank is filled, and monitor your water usage to avoid running out. Use a water pressure regulator to protect your RV's plumbing from excessively high water pressure at the campsite's hookup. When it comes to wastewater, make use of a sewer hose support to ensure proper drainage and prevent any backups.

Safety is a critical aspect of setting up your campsite. Be aware of fire regulations and follow them closely, especially during dry seasons. Set up your campfire in a designated fire pit or ring and maintain a bucket of water or fire extinguisher nearby for safety. Store food securely to prevent attracting wildlife to your campsite, and follow any guidelines or rules provided by the campground or park.

Lastly, be considerate of your fellow campers. Maintain noise levels to a minimum during quiet hours, which are typically enforced at most campgrounds. Dispose of trash in designated containers and recycle when possible. Respect the natural environment and wildlife, and leave no trace of your visit by cleaning up after yourself.

In conclusion, setting up your RV campsite is integral to the RVing experience, and careful preparation is key to a successful and wonderful stay. Choose a suitable location, level and secure your RV, and create a comfortable outdoor space. Be mindful of utilities, safety regulations, and campground etiquette. By following these guidelines, you can make the most of your time in the great outdoors, creating lasting memories as well as experiencing the beauty of nature while enjoying the comforts of your RV.

CHAPTER IV

Navigating the National Parks

Understanding park regulations

RV camping in national and state parks offers a unique chance to connect with nature while enjoying the comforts of home on wheels. However, to ensure a safe and harmonious experience for all visitors and protect the natural beauty of these areas, it is essential to understand and abide by park regulations specific to RV camping. This section will explore the significance of these regulations, common rules and guidelines, and the importance of responsible RV camping within our protected parks.

Park regulations are a set of rules and guidelines established by park authorities to manage and protect the environment, ensure visitor safety, and maintain the quality of the park experience. When it comes to RV camping, these regulations are designed to balance the enjoyment of outdoor enthusiasts with the preservation of natural resources and cultural heritage. Common regulations include restrictions on campsite selection, campfire management, waste disposal, and noise control.

One of the most critical aspects of RV camping regulations is campsite selection. Most parks designate specific areas or campgrounds for RV camping. It is essential to reserve a campsite in advance and to set up your RV only in designated areas. This helps manage the environmental impact of camping and prevents damage to fragile ecosystems and wildlife habitats.

Campfire regulations are also of paramount importance. Many parks have strict rules regarding open fires; some may prohibit them entirely due to fire risk. Understanding and adhering to these regulations helps prevent wildfires, protects the park's vegetation, and ensures the safety of all visitors. If fires are allowed, always use designated fire rings or grills and follow fire safety guidelines.

Waste disposal is another crucial aspect of RV camping regulations. Never dump wastewater or sewage on the ground; instead, use designated dump stations provided by the park or campground. Properly dispose of trash in designated containers to prevent litter and wildlife attraction. Follow recycling guidelines when available to reduce your environmental footprint.

Noise control regulations are in place to maintain the tranquility of the park and minimize disturbances to wildlife and fellow campers. Quiet hours are typically established during the early morning and late evening, during which loud noise and disruptive activities should be avoided. By respecting these regulations, you can contribute to a peaceful and enjoyable atmosphere for all.

Certain parks may have specific regulations related to wildlife interactions. Feeding wildlife is almost always prohibited as it can disrupt natural behaviors and harm animals. Store food securely to prevent attracting wildlife to your campsite, and keep a safe distance from any animals you encounter. Always observe wildlife from a respectful distance and never approach or attempt to feed them.

RV campers need to familiarize themselves with park regulations before their trip. These regulations are typically available on park websites or at visitor centers. Ignorance of the rules is not an excuse for non-compliance, as violations can result in fines, citations, or eviction from the park. By understanding and adhering to these regulations, RV campers can contribute to the conservation of our natural treasures and ensure that future generations can enjoy these beautiful and ecologically significant areas.

In conclusion, understanding park regulations in the context of RV camping is crucial for a responsible and enjoyable outdoor experience. These regulations are in place to protect the environment, ensure visitor safety, and maintain the quality of the park experience. Campers must be aware of rules related to campsite selection, campfires, waste disposal, noise control, and wildlife interactions. By following these guidelines, RV campers can enjoy our parks' beauty while helping preserve them for generations to come. Responsible RV camping is a privilege and a responsibility to protect our protected areas' natural and cultural heritage.

Park entrance fees and passes

RV camping in national and state parks is a fantastic way to experience the beauty of the outdoors while enjoying the comforts of home on the road. While these natural treasures offer endless opportunities for exploration, it's essential to understand the role of park entrance fees and passes in supporting and facilitating these experiences. In this section, we will explore the significance of park entrance fees, the benefits they offer to RV campers, and the various passes available to make these adventures more accessible and affordable.

Park entrance fees play a crucial role in maintaining and preserving the natural and cultural resources of our national and state parks. These fees help fund necessary services such as trail maintenance, visitor centers, restroom facilities, and wildlife management. Without the revenue generated by entrance fees, these services might be compromised, negatively impacting the visitor experience and the conservation of these valuable areas.

One of the primary benefits of park entrance fees is that they grant RV campers access to some of the country's most breathtaking landscapes and outdoor recreational opportunities. These fees open the door to a world of natural wonders, from majestic mountains and pristine lakes to lush forests and unique geological formations. RV campers can confidently explore these remarkable destinations, knowing that their fees contribute to protecting and preserving these cherished places.

To make RV camping more accessible and affordable for visitors, various passes and programs are available. Popular choices include the "America the Beautiful Pass," also known as the America the Beautiful National Parks and Federal Recreational Lands Pass. With this yearly pass, you can visit more than 2,000 federal recreation areas in the US, such as national parks, forests, wildlife refuges, and more. It offers excellent value for RV campers planning to visit multiple sites within a year, making it a cost-effective choice.

The Senior Pass is a valuable option for senior RV campers aged 62 and older. This pass significantly discounts entrance fees and amenities at federal recreation sites. It offers an affordable way for older Americans to explore the beauty and history of our nation's parks, making it an excellent choice for retirees and active seniors.

The Access Pass is designed for U.S. citizens or permanent residents with permanent disabilities. It grants free or discounted access to federal recreation sites and facilities, ensuring that individuals with disabilities can enjoy outdoor experiences like RV camping, hiking, and wildlife watching without financial barriers.

Active-duty military members and their dependents can obtain a free Annual Military Pass, which provides access to the same federal recreation sites covered by the America the Beautiful Pass. This pass is a token of appreciation for the service and sacrifices made by military personnel and their families, allowing them to enjoy outdoor adventures together.

Additionally, the Every Kid Outdoors program offers a free pass to all fourth-grade students, allowing them to explore public lands, waters, and historical sites throughout the school year. This program aims to inspire a love for the outdoors and connect children with the natural and cultural heritage of the United States, fostering a sense of stewardship for these valuable resources from a young age.

In conclusion, park entrance fees and passes are vital in facilitating and supporting RV camping adventures in national and state parks. These fees help maintain and protect these areas' natural and cultural resources, ensuring that they remain accessible and enjoyable for generations to come. RV campers can take advantage of various passes and programs to make their outdoor experiences more affordable and accessible, from the America the Beautiful Pass to senior, disability, military, and youth passes. By supporting these fee programs and taking advantage of available passes, RV campers contribute to preserving our nation's beautiful and ecologically significant public lands.

Navigating park roads and campgrounds

RV camping in national and state parks offers a unique chance to immerse oneself in the beauty of nature while enjoying the comforts of a home on wheels. However, the process of navigating park roads and campgrounds can present some challenges, especially for those new to RV camping. This section will navigate the significance of understanding park road and campground navigation, offer tips for safe and stress-free travel, and discuss the unique considerations when driving and parking an RV.

First and foremost, understanding park road and campground layouts is essential for a successful RV camping experience. Parks vary widely in terms of road conditions, terrain, and the availability of amenities, so it's crucial to research and plan your route in advance. Most parks provide maps and information on their websites, helping RV campers familiarize themselves with the park's layout, including road conditions, campground locations, and any size restrictions or special considerations for RVs.

Safety should always be the top priority when driving an RV in a park. RVs are larger and heavier compared to regular vehicles, needing more time and distance to stop. Keep a safe following distance and be cautious when changing lanes or merging onto park roads. Be aware of low clearances, especially when passing under bridges or entering parking areas.

In addition to safety, it's important to be considerate of other park visitors. Drive at a reasonable speed, especially within campgrounds, to reduce dust, noise, and the risk of accidents. Observe posted speed limits and traffic signs, and always yield the right-of-way when necessary. Be patient and courteous when passing pedestrians, cyclists, or other vehicles on narrow park roads.

Before arriving at your chosen RV campsite, ensure that it is suitable for your RV's size and amenities. Many campgrounds offer different types of sites, including full hookups (electricity, water, and sewer), partial hookups, or no hookups. Ensure your RV has the necessary adapters and extension cords to connect to the available utilities. Be prepared to level your RV using leveling blocks or pads to ensure a comfortable and stable setup.

When parking your RV in a campsite, take care to position it within the designated area and align it properly with utility connections. Remember the space required for slide-outs, awnings, and outdoor furniture. Stabilize your RV by deploying leveling jacks or stabilizer bars as needed. Be mindful of any surrounding vegetation or obstacles that could affect your setup.

Planning ahead for campground amenities and services is also essential. Many campgrounds offer restrooms, showers, laundry facilities, and even camp stores for supplies. Check whether the campground provides a dump station for wastewater disposal or if you'll need to utilize your RV's holding tanks during your stay.

Finally, it's important to respect campground rules and regulations. Most campgrounds have quiet hours to ensure a peaceful atmosphere for all visitors. Follow rules related to campfires, waste disposal, and pet restrictions. To keep everyone safe and comfortable, keep noise levels down during quiet hours and always clean up after your pets.

In conclusion, navigating park roads and campgrounds during RV camping requires careful planning, consideration for safety, and awareness of park rules and regulations. Familiarize yourself with the park's layout, drive cautiously, and be mindful of fellow visitors. Choose a campsite that suits your RV's needs and level it properly. Be prepared to connect to utilities and utilize campground amenities. By following these guidelines, RV campers can enjoy a smooth and enjoyable experience, allowing them to fully appreciate the natural beauty and outdoor adventures that our national and state parks have to offer.

Pet and wildlife guidelines

RV camping allows outdoor enthusiasts to experience the beauty of nature while enjoying the comforts of home on the road. For many campers, pets are an integral part of the family, and the opportunity to explore natural wonders often includes bringing furry companions along.

However, it is essential to understand and follow pet and wildlife guidelines to ensure a safe and respectful camping experience for all. In this section, we will explore the significance of these guidelines, the benefits of responsible pet ownership, and the importance of protecting wildlife in RV camping.

One of the primary reasons for pet and wildlife guidelines in RV camping is to ensure the safety of both pets and humans. National and state parks are diverse ecosystems with varying wildlife populations, including potentially dangerous animals such as bears, cougars, and venomous snakes. Following guidelines related to pet leashing, containment, and supervision helps prevent dangerous encounters and keeps both pets and campers safe.

Responsible pet ownership also extends to protecting the natural environment. Pets can significantly impact fragile ecosystems, disrupting wildlife habitats and endangering plant life. Following guidelines related to waste disposal and wildlife interactions helps minimize the ecological footprint of RV camping. Always clean up after pets, dispose of waste in designated containers, and prevent pets from chasing or disturbing wildlife.

Leash laws are common in many campgrounds and parks to prevent pets from wandering freely and disturbing wildlife or other campers. Ensure that your pet is always on a leash, and keep them within your campsite or designated pet-friendly areas. This not only maintains a respectful camping environment but also prevents pets from getting lost or injured.

Additionally, pet guidelines often specify quiet hours for pets, much like the quiet hours imposed on human campers. Excessive barking or noise from pets can disrupt the peace and tranquility of the campground, affecting the experience of fellow campers. Be mindful of these quiet hours and keep noise levels to a minimum to ensure an enjoyable atmosphere for all.

Wildlife in national and state parks should be observed and admired from a safe distance. It is vital to prevent pets from chasing, approaching, or interacting with wild animals. Such interactions can endanger both pets and wildlife and disrupt natural behaviors. Always keep your pet under control and do not allow them to approach or harass wildlife.

Another crucial aspect of pet and wildlife guidelines is waste management. Proper disposal of pet waste is not only a matter of cleanliness but also an issue of environmental preservation. Pet waste can introduce harmful bacteria into the ecosystem and contaminate water sources. Use designated pet waste disposal facilities or follow campground rules for pet waste disposal to minimize environmental impact.

To protect wildlife, it is essential to store food and garbage securely. Wildlife may be attracted to the scent of food, leading to potential conflicts and habituation to human food sources. Use bear-resistant food containers or follow campground guidelines for food storage to prevent wildlife from accessing your supplies.

In conclusion, pet and wildlife guidelines in RV camping are essential for ensuring a safe, respectful, and environmentally responsible camping experience. Responsible pet ownership involves keeping pets leashed, quiet, and under control, as well as cleaning up after them and preventing interactions with wildlife. Protecting wildlife requires proper food and garbage storage to prevent human-wildlife conflicts. By following these guidelines, RV campers can enjoy the natural beauty and outdoor adventures of our national and state parks while respecting the delicate balance of the ecosystems and preserving the wilderness for future generations.

CHAPTER V

Choosing the Perfect Campsite

Types of campgrounds within national parks

RV camping in national parks offers an exceptional opportunity to immerse oneself in the innate beauty and outdoor adventures that these protected areas provide. National parks boast a variety of campgrounds to accommodate RV campers, each offering a unique experience. In this section, we will explore the different types of campgrounds within national parks, their features, and the considerations for choosing the right one for your RV camping adventure.

Frontcountry campgrounds are typically the most accessible and well-equipped campgrounds within national parks. They are often located near visitor centers, main attractions, and park roads, making them convenient for RV campers. These campgrounds offer various amenities, including RV-friendly campsites with electrical hookups, water, and sewer connections or dump stations. They also provide restrooms, showers, and picnic areas, making them suitable for those who prefer a mix of comfort and nature.

Backcountry campgrounds offer a more rugged and remote RV camping experience. They are typically located deeper within the park and require RV campers to navigate unpaved roads or trails to reach them. Backcountry campgrounds often offer fewer amenities, with some providing only basic pit toilets and no electrical or water hookups. RVs should be well-suited for off-road travel, and campers must be self-sufficient, as these campgrounds may lack the conveniences of frontcountry sites.

Primitive campgrounds are a step beyond backcountry camping, providing minimal facilities and services. RV campers at primitive campgrounds may find themselves in serene and less crowded settings, but these campgrounds usually lack hookups, showers, and flush toilets. Campers must be prepared to rely on their RV's self-contained systems for water and waste management. Primitive campgrounds are ideal for those seeking a more rustic and secluded experience.

Group campgrounds are designed for larger gatherings of RV campers, such as family reunions or group outings. These campgrounds offer multiple campsites, often equipped with fire rings, picnic tables, as well as access to restrooms. Group campgrounds are a great choice for those traveling with several RVs, as they provide a communal atmosphere for socializing while still offering individual sites for privacy.

Equestrian campgrounds cater to RV campers who travel with horses. These campgrounds offer facilities and amenities specifically designed for equestrian enthusiasts, including horse corrals, hitching posts, and access to horse-friendly trails. RV campers with horses can enjoy the convenience of being close to equestrian activities while still having access to basic camping facilities.

Some national parks offer campgrounds situated in scenic locations that provide stunning vistas of natural wonders such as mountains, canyons, lakes, or rivers. RV campers who prioritize breathtaking views and proximity to iconic landmarks may choose these campgrounds, even if they offer fewer amenities. The trade-off is often worth it for the opportunity to wake up to awe-inspiring vistas right outside your RV.

When choosing a campground within a national park for your RV camping adventure, consider your preferences and priorities. Do you value convenience and comfort, or are you seeking a more rugged and remote experience? Are you traveling with horses or a large group? Do you prioritize scenic views and proximity to attractions? By understanding the types of campgrounds available and their features, RV campers can make informed decisions that enhance their national park camping experience and create lasting memories in the great outdoors.

Reservation strategies

Planning an RV camping trip to national or state parks is an exciting adventure, but it's crucial to have a solid reservation strategy in place to secure your ideal campsite and make the most of your outdoor experience. In this section, we will explore reservation strategies for RV camping, including when and how to make reservations, tips for popular destinations, and the benefits of planning ahead.

One of the most critical aspects of a successful RV camping trip is making reservations well in advance. Many national and state parks are highly sought-after destinations, and their campgrounds can fill up quickly, especially during peak seasons. To increase your chances of securing a campsite that suits your preferences and needs, it's advisable to make reservations as early as possible.

The timing of your reservation depends on the specific park and its reservation system. Most national parks allow reservations up to six months in advance, while some state parks may offer a more extended booking window. Be sure to check the reservation policies of the park you plan to visit and mark the opening date for reservations on your calendar. Set a reminder to log in or call the reservation system as soon as it opens to secure your spot.

For highly popular parks or campgrounds, making a reservation on the first day it becomes available is often crucial. Many campers set alarms to ensure they are ready to book their desired dates and sites promptly. Keep in mind that prime camping dates, such as holidays and weekends, tend to fill up fastest, so planning early is particularly important for these occasions.

Researching and selecting the right campsite for your RV is another crucial part of the reservation process. National and state park campgrounds offer various types of sites, including those with full hookups, partial hookups, or no hookups at all. Consider your RV's size and needs when choosing a campsite. Full-hookup sites provide convenience with water, electricity, and sewer connections, while no-hookup sites offer a more rustic experience for self-contained RVs.

It's also important to read campground reviews and look at photos to get a sense of the campsite's amenities, views, and proximity to attractions. Factors like shade, privacy, and ease of access can greatly influence your camping experience. Keep in mind that some campgrounds within parks may have restrictions on RV length or generator use, so be sure to check the specific campground rules.

Flexibility is key when making reservations for RV camping. If your preferred dates or campsite are not available, consider adjusting your travel plans. Mid-week stays or visits during the shoulder season can often provide a more relaxed camping experience and better availability. Alternatively, explore nearby campgrounds or parks that may offer similar experiences.

Having a backup plan is also a wise strategy. In case your first-choice campground is fully booked, identify alternative campgrounds within the same park or nearby areas. This allows you to adjust your itinerary and still enjoy the innate beauty and outdoor activities of the region.

Lastly, consider the benefits of booking multiple campgrounds if you plan to visit multiple destinations during your RV camping trip. This approach allows you to secure your preferred sites at each location and ensures a smoother travel experience.

In conclusion, reservation strategies are a critical component of a successful RV camping trip. Making reservations well in advance, researching campsite options, and planning for flexibility are key elements of a robust strategy. By following these guidelines and staying organized, RV campers can secure their ideal campsites, enjoy the great outdoors, and create unforgettable memories while exploring national and state parks.

Campground amenities and facilities

Recreational Vehicle (RV) camping has gained immense popularity in recent years, attracting outdoor enthusiasts and travelers seeking adventure and comfort. As a result, campgrounds have evolved to cater to the unique needs of RV campers by providing an array of amenities and facilities to enhance the camping experience. These amenities not only provide convenience and comfort but also make RV camping an attractive option for individuals and families alike.

One of the most crucial aspects of RV camping is access to reliable electrical hookups. Most RVs are equipped with appliances and gadgets that require electricity to function properly. Campgrounds typically provide 30-amp or 50-amp electrical hookups, ensuring that campers can power their RVs and enjoy the comforts of home while in the great outdoors. These hookups enable campers to run air conditioning units, charge electronic devices, and use kitchen appliances without worrying about power shortages.

Water and sewage facilities are another vital component of campground amenities. RVs come equipped with freshwater tanks and waste holding tanks, but access to potable water and sewage disposal services is essential for an extended camping stay. Campgrounds offer water hookups, allowing RV campers to fill their freshwater tanks easily. Furthermore, many campgrounds provide dump stations or full hookups, allowing campers to dispose of their wastewater conveniently and maintain a clean and hygienic camping environment.

To make the RV camping experience more enjoyable, many campgrounds provide amenities such as showers and restrooms. Clean and well-maintained shower as well as restroom facilities are highly appreciated by campers, providing them with a comfortable and hygienic space to freshen up after a day of outdoor activities. These amenities are especially valuable for campers traveling in smaller RVs that may have limited bathroom facilities onboard.

In addition to essential utilities, campgrounds often provide recreational amenities to enhance the overall camping experience. Many campgrounds feature recreational areas with playgrounds for children, picnic areas for family gatherings, and outdoor grilling stations for campers who prefer to cook outdoors. Some campgrounds even offer swimming pools, hot tubs, and fitness centers to help campers relax and stay active during their stay.

For those who prefer to stay connected while on the road, Wi-Fi access is becoming increasingly common in campgrounds. Having an access to the internet can be crucial for work, communication, or entertainment purposes, making Wi-Fi a valuable amenity for RV campers. Additionally, some campgrounds offer cable TV hookups so that campers can enjoy their favorite shows and stay updated on news and events.

Safety and security are paramount concerns for RV campers, and many campgrounds take measures to ensure the well-being of their guests. Gated entrances, security patrols, and well-lit areas are some of the security features that campgrounds may provide to create a safe and comfortable camping environment. Furthermore, campgrounds often organize events and activities to foster a sense of community among campers. These events can include outdoor movie nights, campfire gatherings, potluck dinners, and nature hikes. Such activities allow campers to socialize with fellow travelers and create lasting memories while enjoying the beauty of the great outdoors.

In conclusion, campground amenities and facilities for RV camping play a crucial role in enhancing the overall camping experience. From essential utilities like electrical hookups and water facilities to recreational amenities, Wi-Fi access, and security measures, campgrounds strive to provide RV campers with comfort, convenience, and a sense of community. These amenities make RV camping a popular and enjoyable way to navigate the outdoors while maintaining the comforts of home. Whether you are a seasoned RV enthusiast or a newcomer to the world of RV camping, the availability of these amenities ensures that your camping experience is both memorable and satisfying.

Finding off-the-beaten-path spots

RV camping offers the freedom to explore diverse landscapes, immerse oneself in nature, and discover hidden gems that may not be on the common tourist map. While popular tourist destinations have their merits, there's a unique charm in venturing off the beaten path and uncovering secluded spots that provide a deeper connection with the great outdoors. In this section, we will explore the joys of finding off-the-beaten-path locations during RV camping and offer tips on how to discover these hidden treasures.

One of the most significant advantages of RV camping is the flexibility it offers. Unlike traditional accommodations, RVs provide the opportunity to change your travel plans on a whim. When planning an RV trip, consider researching less-traveled routes or remote areas that pique your interest. National parks, state forests, and remote campgrounds often offer unspoiled natural beauty and solitude that are worth exploring. Consult maps, travel guides, and online forums to identify potential off-the-beaten-path destinations in your chosen region.

Local knowledge can be invaluable when seeking hidden spots. Engaging with locals or fellow RV travelers can lead to invaluable insights and recommendations. Strike up conversations at campgrounds, visit local cafes or shops, and ask for advice from those who know the area best. They might point you towards lesser-known hiking trails, pristine lakes, or charming small towns that are not part of the typical tourist circuit.

Embrace the spirit of spontaneity when RV camping.

While it's essential to have a general plan in place, allow room for detours and unexpected discoveries. Keep an eye out for intriguing road signs, scenic viewpoints, or intriguing landmarks that invite exploration. Some of the most memorable experiences during RV camping occur when you decide to take a turn down an unfamiliar road or follow a trail that piques your curiosity.

Technology can be a helpful ally in your quest to find off-the-beaten-path spots. GPS devices, navigation apps, and online resources provide a wealth of information about remote and lesser-known locations. Websites and apps dedicated to RV travel often feature user-generated content and reviews, which can offer valuable insights into hidden gems. Utilize these tools to plan your route and identify intriguing stops along the way.

When venturing off the beaten path, it's essential to be prepared. Remote locations may lack the amenities and services that more popular tourist destinations provide. Ensure that your RV is well-equipped with essential supplies, including food, water, and camping gear. Consider carrying a first-aid kit, extra fuel, and a generator if needed. Check your RV's maintenance to avoid unexpected breakdowns in remote areas. Having a well-stocked and well-maintained RV will provide peace of mind during your off-the-beaten-path adventures.

Responsible and eco-conscious RV camping is crucial when exploring less-traveled areas. Practice Leave No Trace principles by reducing your impact on the environment. Dispose of waste properly, respect wildlife and natural habitats, and follow local regulations and guidelines. By leaving these hidden spots as pristine as you found them, you contribute to their preservation for future generations to enjoy.

In conclusion, RV camping provides an excellent opportunity to uncover off-the-beaten-path spots that offer solitude, natural beauty, and authentic experiences. With proper planning, local knowledge, spontaneity, technology, and responsible camping practices, you can embark on unforgettable journeys to remote and less-traveled destinations. The thrill of discovering hidden treasures during your RV adventures adds a unique dimension to your camping experiences, making them more enriching and memorable. So, as you plan your next RV trip, consider venturing off the beaten path and embracing the unknown, for it is in these hidden corners of the world that you may find the most profound connection with nature and yourself.

CHAPTER VI

Outdoor Activities and Adventures

Hiking trails and tips

RV camping and hiking make for an ideal combination, allowing outdoor enthusiasts to explore the charm of nature while enjoying the comfort and convenience of their home on wheels. Whether you're an experienced hiker or a novice looking to embark on your first trail, there are plenty of opportunities to lace up your hiking boots and hit the trails while RV camping. In this section, we'll explore the joys of hiking during RV camping and provide some valuable tips to make your hiking adventures secure and rewarding.

One of the key benefits of RV camping is the proximity it offers to a wide range of hiking trails. Campgrounds are often located in or near areas of natural beauty, such as national parks, state forests, and wilderness areas, providing easy access to hiking opportunities. Before setting out on a hike, research the trails available in the vicinity of your campground. Many campgrounds provide trail maps and information to help you plan your adventure. Additionally, websites, apps, and guidebooks dedicated to hiking are valuable resources for finding trails suitable for your skill level and preferences.

When selecting a hiking trail, consider your fitness level and the capabilities of your hiking companions. Trails differ in difficulty, from easy walks suitable for families with young children to strenuous hikes that challenge even experienced hikers. Consider the elevation gain, distance, and terrain of the trail to ensure it aligns with your abilities and expectations. If you're unsure, start with shorter, less challenging hikes and gradually work your way up to more strenuous ones as your confidence and stamina grow.

Proper gear and preparation are necessary for a safe and enjoyable hiking experience. Begin by wearing comfortable, moisture-wicking clothing and sturdy hiking boots that provide support and traction. Pack a backpack with essential items, including water, snacks, a first-aid kit, a map or GPS device, a flashlight, a multi-tool, and a fully charged cell phone. Dress in layers, as weather conditions can shift rapidly in many hiking areas. In case of emergency, it's also a good practice to let someone know your hiking plans, including your intended route and your estimated return time.

Respect for nature and Leave No Trace principles should guide your behavior on the trail. Stay on designated paths to minimize damage to the environment, avoid disturbing wildlife, and refrain from littering. Pack out all the trash and waste, including biodegradable items like food scraps. Use established campsites if you plan to camp along the trail, and follow fire regulations if you intend to cook or have a campfire. Complying to these principles helps preserve the natural beauty of hiking areas for future generations.

When hiking during RV camping, you must be aware of your surroundings and be prepared for unexpected situations. Stay on the lookout for trail markers and pay attention to your surroundings to avoid getting lost. Keep an eye on the weather, and be prepared to turn back if conditions deteriorate. If you encounter wildlife, observe from a safe distance and avoid approaching or feeding animals. In remote areas, carry a bear canister or bear spray for added safety.

Finally, take time to savor the experience and immerse yourself in the beauty of nature. Hiking is not only about reaching a destination but also about enjoying the journey. Pause to appreciate scenic vistas, listen to the sounds of nature, and embrace the sense of tranquility that hiking can provide. Carry a camera or smartphone to capture your hiking adventures' breathtaking views and memories.

In conclusion, hiking trails complement your RV camping experience, allowing you to connect with nature and explore the great outdoors. By researching trails, assessing their suitability, preparing properly, and practicing responsible hiking habits, you can make the most of your RV camping hiking adventures. Hiking offers a world of opportunities to explore new landscapes and make enduring memories, whether you're looking for a leisurely stroll or a strenuous ascent. So, as you plan your next RV camping trip, don't forget to pack your hiking gear and explore the trails that await you in nature's embrace.

Wildlife watching

RV camping offers a unique opportunity to immerse oneself in the natural world and connect with the wildlife that inhabits the great outdoors. Whether you're a dedicated birdwatcher, an avid animal enthusiast, or simply a nature lover, there are lots of opportunities to observe and appreciate the diverse wildlife that can be found in various camping destinations. In this section, we'll explore the joys of wildlife watching during RV camping and provide some valuable tips for a rewarding and responsible experience.

One of the most appealing aspects of RV camping is the chance to camp in or near natural habitats that are home to a wide variety of wildlife species. From majestic elk in national parks to elusive birds in remote forests, each camping destination offers a unique opportunity to encounter animals in their natural environment. Research the area you plan to visit to learn about the native wildlife and their habits, as this knowledge will enhance your wildlife-watching experience.

To maximize your opportunities of spotting wildlife during RV camping, it's essential to be patient and observant. Animals are frequently the most active during dawn and dusk, so plan your wildlife-watching excursions accordingly. Use binoculars or spotting scopes to watch animals from a safe distance, minimizing disturbance to their natural behavior. Keep noise to a minimum, as loud conversations or the sound of engines can startle or scare away wildlife.

Camouflage clothing and neutral colors can help you blend into your surroundings and avoid attracting unnecessary attention from wildlife. Move slowly and quietly, using cover when possible to approach animals cautiously. Be respectful of their space and boundaries, and never approach or feed the wild animals, as this can damage their natural behavior and be harmful to both the animals and humans.

When wildlife watching, it's crucial to prioritize safety for both yourself and the animals. Maintain a safe distance, especially when observing large or potentially dangerous animals. Some wildlife can become aggressive if they feel threatened or cornered, so always give them space to move freely. If you meet a wild animal that appears sick or injured, it's best to contact local wildlife authorities or rangers rather than attempting to intervene yourself.

Photography can be a rewarding aspect of wildlife watching during RV camping. If you're interested in capturing images of the wildlife you encounter, invest in a telephoto lens to keep a safe distance while getting close-up shots. Remember to respect the animals' space and not disrupt their behavior for the sake of a photograph. Additionally, be mindful of the use of flash photography, as it can startle or distress animals.

To enhance your wildlife-watching experience during RV camping, consider bringing field guides or wildlife identification books to help you identify the species you encounter. You can also use smartphone apps designed for bird and animal identification, which often provide valuable information about the creatures you observe.

Remember that wildlife watching is a form of ecotourism that comes with responsibilities. By practicing ethical and responsible wildlife-watching habits, you contribute to the conservation and protection of the natural environment and the creatures that call it home. Abide by local regulations and guidelines, and avoid disturbing sensitive habitats or nesting areas.

In conclusion, wildlife watching adds a rich and immersive dimension to the RV camping experience, allowing you to connect with the natural world and appreciate the charm of the animals that inhabit it. By preparing properly, being patient and observant, and respecting the animals' space and needs, you can enjoy a rewarding and responsible wildlife-watching experience. Whether you're seeking to spot a rare bird, glimpse a majestic mammal, or simply marvel at the wonders of the natural world, RV camping provides the perfect backdrop for your wildlife adventures. So, as you plan your next RV camping trip, don't forget to pack your binoculars and camera, and prepare to be captivated by the wildlife wonders that await you in the great outdoors.

Fishing and boating opportunities

RV camping provides the perfect platform for outdoor enthusiasts to explore a wide range of recreational activities, and among the most popular are fishing and boating. Whether you're an experienced angler or just looking to relax on the water, there are abundant opportunities to enjoy these activities while RV camping. In this section, we will explore the joys of fishing and boating during RV camping and provide valuable insights into how to make the most of these aquatic adventures.

Fishing is a beloved pastime for many RV campers, and it's easy to see why. RV campgrounds are often located near lakes, rivers, streams, and coastal areas that offer excellent fishing opportunities. Before heading out to your selected fishing spot, it's essential to research local fishing regulations, including license requirements and catch limits. Many campgrounds provide information on nearby fishing locations and can advise you on the best times to fish and the variety of fish you can expect to catch.

RVers can enjoy a wide variety of fishing styles, from fly fishing in pristine mountain streams to casting for bass in tranquil lakes. It's essential to have the right equipment for your chosen fishing method, including fishing rods, reels, lines, bait, and tackle. If you're new to fishing or don't want to invest in equipment, consider local fishing guides or rental services that can provide the necessary gear and expert guidance to ensure a successful fishing experience.

Boating is another popular activity that pairs seamlessly with RV camping, especially when campgrounds are situated near bodies of water. RVers often bring their boats or rent them at nearby marinas to explore lakes, rivers, and coastal areas. Whether you prefer kayaking, canoeing, paddleboarding, or motorized boating, there's something for everyone when it comes to boating opportunities.

When embarking on a boating adventure during RV camping, safety should be a top priority. Ensure that your boat is in good condition and equipped with life jackets, navigation lights, and essential safety equipment. Familiarize yourself with local boating regulations and guidelines, including speed limits, no-wake zones, and restricted areas. Respect wildlife and the natural habitats, and dispose of trash properly to maintain the pristine beauty of the waterways.

Fishing from a boat adds an extra layer of excitement to your angling experience. It allows you to access deeper waters and explore remote fishing spots that may be less accessible from shore. While fishing from a boat, it's crucial to be well-prepared with the right fishing gear and tackle. Additionally, having a fish finder or sonar equipment can be advantageous for locating fish beneath the water's surface.

For those who prefer a more leisurely approach to boating, activities like canoeing and kayaking provide a tranquil way to explore scenic waterways. These non-motorized watercraft allow you to immerse yourself in nature, quietly observe wildlife, and navigate narrow channels and serene coves. Many campgrounds offer kayak and canoe rentals, making it easy for RV campers to enjoy these experiences without the need to transport their boats.

RV campers who enjoy coastal destinations have the opportunity to engage in saltwater fishing and boating. Coastal areas often provide opportunities for deep-sea fishing charters, where you can target larger species such as tuna, marlin, or grouper. Additionally, coastal regions offer the chance to explore tidal estuaries, salt marshes, and coastal bays, providing a unique ecosystem for fishing and boating enthusiasts.

In conclusion, fishing and boating opportunities abound during RV camping, offering a wealth of aquatic experiences for outdoor enthusiasts. Whether you're seeking the thrill of catching a trophy fish, the tranquility of paddling on serene waters, or the adventure of exploring coastal regions, RV camping provides the ideal basecamp for your aquatic adventures. By adhering to safety regulations, respecting the environment, and preparing adequately with the right equipment, you can make the most of your fishing and boating experiences while RV camping. So, as you plan your next RV camping trip, be sure to pack your fishing gear or boat, and get ready to cast your line or set sail on the waterways that await you in the great outdoors.

Ranger-led programs and guided tours

One of the most enriching aspects of RV camping is a chance to absorb oneself in the natural and cultural wonders of the destinations visited. While exploring national and state parks, forests, and other outdoor areas, RV campers can enhance their experience by participating in ranger-led programs and guided tours. These programs offer a more profound understanding of the history, natural environment, and culture of the region, making the camping experience both educational and unforgettable. In this section, we will delve into the value of ranger-led programs and guided tours during RV camping and highlight how they can elevate your camping adventure.

Ranger-led programs are educational and interactive activities conducted by park rangers or naturalists. These programs are designed to engage campers of all ages and provide insights into the ecology, geology, and wildlife of the area. Whether it's a guided hike, an informative talk, a wildlife viewing session, or a stargazing program, ranger-led activities offer a chance to connect with the natural world on a deeper level. Many campgrounds within national and state parks have visitor centers where you can inquire about the schedule of ranger-led programs during your stay.

Participating in ranger-led programs can be especially valuable for families with children. These programs are not only educational but also entertaining, making learning about nature and history fun and engaging. Children can discover the wonders of the outdoors through hands-on activities, interactive demonstrations, and wildlife encounters led by knowledgeable rangers. Moreover, ranger-led programs often provide opportunities for campers to earn badges, certificates, or junior ranger credentials, encouraging a lifelong love of nature and conservation.

Guided tours offer a different perspective on the camping experience, focusing on the cultural and historical aspects of the destination. Whether exploring ancient ruins, historic sites, or heritage trails, guided tours provide a glimpse into the past and the people who shaped the region. Knowledgeable guides offer in-depth information, anecdotes, and stories that bring history to life and make the experience more engaging and meaningful.

When planning an RV camping trip, it's a good idea to research the availability of ranger-led programs and guided tours in the area you intend to visit. Many national and state parks offer a wide range of programs that cater to distinct interests and age groups. Popular topics include wildlife viewing, geology, astronomy, archaeology, and cultural history. Some programs require reservations, so it's advisable to plan ahead and secure your spot, especially during peak camping seasons.

Guided tours can be especially enriching when exploring areas with unique cultural or historical significance. For example, visiting a historic battlefield with a knowledgeable guide can provide a deep understanding of the events that unfolded there. Similarly, exploring indigenous cultural sites with indigenous guides can offer a perspective that goes beyond typical tourist experiences.

Ranger-led programs and guided tours not only enhance your understanding of the natural and cultural heritage but also foster a sense of community among campers. These activities provide opportunities to meet fellow RVers, share experiences, and learn from one another.

Many campers find that participating in ranger-led programs or guided tours creates lasting memories and fosters a sense of appreciation for the environment and the rich tapestry of human history.

In conclusion, ranger-led programs and guided tours are valuable additions to the RV camping experience, offering opportunities for education, enrichment, and a deeper connection with the natural and cultural world. By taking advantage of these programs, RV campers can gain a deeper comprehension of the places they visit and create memorable experiences that go beyond the typical camping trip. So, as you plan your next RV camping adventure, be sure to explore the ranger-led programs and guided tours available in your chosen destinations, and prepare to embark on a journey of discovery and enlightenment in the great outdoors.

CHAPTER VII

RV-Friendly Cooking

Kitchen essentials

RV camping provides the best of both worlds - the freedom to travel and explore while still enjoying the comforts of home. One of the key aspects of feeling at home in your RV is having a well-equipped kitchen. Having the right kitchen essentials can make an important difference in your RV camping experience. In this section, we will explore the essential items you need to equip your RV kitchen, ensuring that you can prepare delicious meals and enjoy the convenience of cooking on the road.

First and foremost, it's crucial to have cookware that suits the limited space and capabilities of an RV kitchen. Opt for non-stick pots and pans that are versatile and easy to clean. A small selection of pots and pans in various sizes, along with a frying pan, should cover most of your cooking needs. Don't forget to include a set of oven mitts or pot holders to secure your hands when handling hot cookware.

To complement your cookware, invest in quality kitchen utensils. Essentials like a chef's knife, paring knife, cutting board, and a set of cooking utensils (spatula, ladle, tongs, etc.) are indispensable for meal preparation. Consider utensils made of durable and heat-resistant materials, and choose items that are compact and easy to store in your RV kitchen.

Food storage is another critical aspect of RV camping. Having a selection of airtight containers, resealable bags, and food storage bins helps keep your ingredients fresh and organized. Additionally, consider purchasing stackable or collapsible storage containers to save space in your RV kitchen cabinets.

No RV kitchen is complete without essential appliances. A compact microwave, a toaster or toaster oven, and a coffee maker are common appliances that can make meal preparation and mornings more convenient. If you're a coffee lover, a portable French press or coffee percolator can be a great addition for brewing your favorite morning brew.

Refrigeration is vital for storing perishable items. Most RVs come equipped with a refrigerator, but it's essential to ensure it's in good working order before your trip. Consider a portable refrigerator or cooler if you need extra storage space for longer journeys or when camping off the grid. Don't forget to stock up on ice packs or ice cubes to keep items cold in the cooler.

Properly equipped RV kitchens also include a selection of cookware and kitchen gadgets. A propane or electric stove with multiple burners permits you to cook an array of dishes. Many RVs also come with ovens for baking. It's advisable to have a selection of mixing bowls, measuring cups and spoons, and a can opener. If you enjoy grilling, an outdoor barbecue or portable grill can be a valuable addition to your camping gear.

Dishwashing is a crucial task in any kitchen, and RV camping is no exception. Ensure you have biodegradable dish soap, sponges, scrubbers, and dish towels to clean your cookware and utensils. Consider a collapsible dishpan or drying rack to save space and make dishwashing more manageable.

Finally, don't forget about safety. Every RV kitchen should be equipped with a fire extinguisher and a basic first-aid kit. Ensure that your RV's smoke and carbon monoxide detectors are functioning correctly, as safety is paramount when cooking in confined spaces.

In conclusion, equipping your RV kitchen with essential items is crucial for a successful as well as enjoyable camping experience. Having the right cookware, utensils, appliances, and storage solutions can make cooking and meal preparation in your RV convenient and comfortable. By ensuring that your RV kitchen is well-equipped, you can savor delicious home-cooked meals while on the road and make the most of your RV camping adventure. So, before embarking on your next RV trip, take the time to stock your kitchen with the essentials, and prepare to create culinary delights in the heart of nature.

Meal planning and recipes

RV camping is a wonderful way to navigate the great outdoors while also enjoying the comforts of home on wheels. One essential aspect of RV camping is meal planning and preparing delicious meals that can be enjoyed in the midst of nature. With a well-thought-out meal plan and a repertoire of easy and tasty recipes, you can make your RV camping experience not only convenient but also memorable.

To begin with, meal planning for RV camping requires careful consideration of your camping location, the duration of your trip, and the available kitchen facilities in your RV. It's important to plan meals that are not only convenient to prepare but also suitable for the environment. Since space is often limited in RV kitchens, it's best to focus on recipes that require minimal equipment and utensils. Consider dishes that can be prepared in one pot or on a single burner, which will help save time and reduce the need for extensive cleanup.

Breakfast is the most important meal of the day, and RV campers can start their day right with easy-to-make and energizing breakfast recipes. Classics like scrambled eggs with vegetables or breakfast burritos are quick to prepare and can be customized to individual preferences. If you prefer something sweet, you can whip up pancakes or French toast with a selection of toppings like berries, syrup, or powdered sugar. These breakfast options are not only delicious but also filling, ensuring you have the energy you need for a day of outdoor adventures.

For lunch, consider creating simple yet satisfying sandwiches or wraps. Cold cuts, cheese, and a variety of condiments can be easily stored in the RV refrigerator and used to make quick and customizable sandwiches. Alternatively, prepare some hearty salads with pre-chopped veggies and canned beans or tuna. These options are not only healthy but also easy to assemble, allowing you to get back to enjoying the great outdoors in no time.

When it comes to dinner, one-pot or one-pan recipes are a camper's best friend. A hearty chili, stew, or pasta dish can be cooked in a single pot, minimizing the amount of cookware needed and making cleanup a breeze. Many RVs come equipped with a stovetop and an oven, allowing for more culinary versatility. Roasting vegetables, baking casseroles, or grilling meat or fish can provide you with a diverse range of dinner options. Don't forget to bring along spices, herbs, and seasonings to add flavor to your meals.

Snacking is an essential part of any camping trip, and RV campers can keep their energy levels up with a selection of healthy snacks. Nuts, dried fruits, granola bars, and fresh fruits are easy to store and provide quick and nutritious pick-me-ups throughout the day.

As for beverages, it's important to stay hydrated while camping. Ensure you have an ample supply of water and consider bringing along a portable water filtration system for freshwater sources you may encounter during your journey. Additionally, bring your favorite beverages, such as coffee or tea, to enjoy the comforts of your preferred morning ritual while in the great outdoors.

In conclusion, meal planning and recipes for RV camping are all about convenience, simplicity, and taste. With the proper preparation and a bit of creativity, you can enjoy delicious meals while immersing yourself in the beauty of nature. Whether you're a seasoned RV camper or new to the adventure, a well-planned menu will enhance your camping experience and make it even more enjoyable. So, pack your RV kitchen essentials, plan your meals, and get ready to savor the flavors of the wilderness on your next RV camping trip.

Outdoor cooking equipment

When embarking on an RV camping adventure, one of the most exciting aspects is the opportunity to cook and enjoy delicious meals amidst the beauty of the great outdoors. To make the most of this experience, it's essential to have the right outdoor cooking equipment at your disposal. Whether you're a seasoned camper or new to RVing, having the appropriate gear can enhance your culinary adventures and ensure that you and your fellow campers can savor the flavors of the wilderness.

One of the fundamental pieces of outdoor cooking equipment for RV camping is a reliable camping stove. These stoves come in various types, including propane, butane, and multi-fuel stoves. Propane stoves are a popular choice for RV campers due to their efficiency and ease of use. They provide consistent heat and are capable of accommodating different cookware sizes. Butane stoves are also portable and easy to operate, making them suitable for smaller RV kitchens. Multi-fuel stoves provide versatility by allowing you to use different types of fuel, such as white gas, kerosene, or unleaded gasoline, depending on availability.

Another indispensable tool for outdoor cooking is a set of quality cookware. Lightweight and durable pots, pans, and utensils are essential for preparing a variety of meals. Non-stick cookware is particularly advantageous for RV camping, as it simplifies both cooking and cleaning. Ensure that your cookware is appropriately sized for your RV's stove and oven to maximize efficiency.

To complement your cookware, consider investing in a set of outdoor cooking utensils. Long-handled spatulas, tongs, and ladles are invaluable for safe and easy cooking over an open flame or on a camping stove. A set of sharp knives and a cutting board are also essential for food preparation. Opt for utensils and tools designed for outdoor use, as they are often more durable and heat-resistant than their indoor counterparts.

A portable barbecue grill is an excellent complement to your outdoor cooking gear if you're a griller. Propane or charcoal grills are popular choices, providing the opportunity to grill burgers, steaks, vegetables, and more. Some RVs come equipped with built-in grills, while others may require a portable option that can be set up outside.

An often overlooked but crucial piece of equipment is a fire extinguisher. Safety should always be a top priority when cooking outdoors, and having a fire extinguisher on hand can provide peace of mind in case of emergencies. Be sure to familiarize yourself with its proper use and keep it quickly accessible in case of need.

To make outdoor cooking even more enjoyable, consider adding some creature comforts to your RV kitchen. A portable table or camp kitchen can provide extra workspace and storage for your cooking equipment and ingredients. An outdoor canopy or awning can provide shade as well as protection from the elements, allowing you to cook comfortably in various weather conditions.

Lastly, don't forget about the importance of food storage. Adequate coolers or refrigerators in your RV can keep perishable items fresh during your camping trip. Consider using storage containers or vacuum-sealed bags to keep food organized and prevent any unwanted critters from invading your supplies.

In conclusion, outdoor cooking equipment for RV camping is essential for a successful as well as enjoyable trip. Whether you're a fan of stovetop cooking, grilling, or both, having the right gear can make all the difference in your culinary adventures. With the appropriate camping stove, cookware, utensils, and safety equipment, you can create memorable meals and savor the joys of cooking in the great outdoors while RV camping. So, pack your kitchen essentials, gear up for your next adventure, and prepare to indulge in the delightful tastes of the wilderness.

Dining etiquette in the wilderness

RV camping is a wonderful way to connect with nature, but it also requires a certain level of respect for the environment and your fellow campers. This includes practicing good dining etiquette when enjoying meals in the wilderness. While it may not be as formal as a fine-dining experience, adhering to some basic principles can enhance your camping trip and help maintain a harmonious outdoor atmosphere.

First and foremost, cleanliness is paramount when it comes to dining etiquette in the wilderness. Always clean up after yourself, whether you're cooking at your campsite or dining at a communal picnic area. Dispose of food scraps, trash, and packaging properly in designated receptacles or by following Leave No Trace principles if no facilities are available. This not only keeps the campsite tidy but also helps protect wildlife from ingesting harmful substances.

When cooking and eating outdoors, be mindful of the local wildlife. Avoid feeding wildlife, as it can damage their natural behaviors and lead to potentially dangerous encounters. Keep all food securely stored in airtight containers or coolers to prevent animals from being attracted to your campsite. Additionally, respect any posted regulations or guidelines related to wildlife interaction in the area.

In a communal camping setting, such as a campground with designated picnic areas, be considerate of other campers. Keep noise levels down during meal times to avoid disturbing those nearby who may be seeking tranquility. Use designated cooking and dining areas when available, and avoid encroaching on others' campsites. If you're playing music or have other forms of entertainment, be sure the volume is at a level that doesn't intrude on your neighbors' peace and quiet. Proper

disposal of wastewater is essential in maintaining the wilderness's cleanliness. When washing dishes, use biodegradable soap and a small basin to collect the water. Dispose of the wastewater away from water sources, following any specific guidelines provided by the campground. This helps prevent contamination of rivers, lakes, and streams, ensuring that they remain pristine for all to enjoy.

Respect the natural surroundings while dining in the wilderness. Avoid damaging vegetation by setting up your cooking and dining area on durable surfaces like gravel or bare ground. Do not pick plants or disturb the natural landscape. It's also essential to follow fire regulations and only use designated fire rings or stoves for cooking. Never leave a campfire unattended and guarantee it is completely extinguished before leaving the site.

When dining with fellow campers, practice good campfire and mealtime etiquette. Share the responsibilities of meal preparation and cleanup, and offer to help others if needed. Keep conversations enjoyable and inclusive, and be mindful of sensitive topics that may be inappropriate in a diverse group setting. If you have pets, ensure they are well-behaved and considerate of others.

Lastly, be aware of local regulations and guidelines specific to the area where you are camping. Different parks, forests, and campgrounds may have their own rules regarding outdoor dining, campfires, and waste disposal. Familiarize yourself with these regulations and follow them diligently to avoid any legal or environmental issues.

In conclusion, dining etiquette in the wilderness during RV camping is not just about following a set of rules; it's about showing respect for the environment, wildlife, and fellow campers. By keeping your campsite clean, minimizing noise, and following local regulations, you can contribute to a more enjoyable and harmonious outdoor experience for yourself and others. Good dining etiquette enhances the joy of RV camping while ensuring that the wilderness remains a pristine and inviting place for generations to come.

CHAPTER VIII

Staying Connected on the Road

Internet and communication options

In today's connected world, staying in touch and having access to the internet while RV camping has become increasingly important for many travelers. Whether you're a full-time RVer or just enjoy occasional RV trips, having reliable communication options can enhance your overall camping experience. Fortunately, there are many ways to remain connected as well as access the internet while on the road.

One of the most common options for internet and communication during RV camping is through cellular networks. Most RVs come equipped with cell phones and data plans, allowing you to use your smartphone as a hotspot to provide internet access to your other devices. This method works well in areas with good cellular coverage, and it's convenient for checking emails, social media, and staying connected with loved ones. However, it's essential to be aware that cellular signal strength can differ depending on your location, and you may encounter dead zones in remote areas.

For those who require more robust and consistent internet connectivity, consider investing in a dedicated mobile hotspot device or a cellular signal booster. Mobile hotspots are compact devices that provide a Wi-Fi network using cellular data, and they often offer better performance than using your smartphone as a hotspot. Cellular signal boosters, on the other hand, can enhance the strength of your existing cellular signal, making it more reliable and faster.

Satellite internet is another option for RV campers who venture into areas with limited cellular coverage. While satellite internet can be expensive and may require professional installation, it offers a reliable connection even in remote locations where cellular networks are scarce. However, the equipment can be bulky, and signal latency can be an issue, making it less suitable for real-time activities such as online gaming or video conferencing.

Many RV campgrounds and parks offer Wi-Fi access to their guests, which can be a convenient option for staying connected while camping. Keep in mind that the quality and speed of campground Wi-Fi can vary widely. In some cases, it may be suitable for basic tasks such as checking emails as well as browsing the web, while in others, it may be slow and unreliable, especially during peak usage times. Certain campgrounds might impose a fee for using the Wi-Fi or place limits on how much data you can use.

Another popular option for communication during RV camping is two-way radios or walkie-talkies. These devices are handy for staying in touch with fellow campers when exploring large campgrounds, hiking trails, or participating in outdoor activities. They are typically rugged, portable, and don't require cellular coverage.

If you prefer a more traditional means of communication, consider a satellite phone. Satellite phones can provide reliable voice communication in remote areas where cell signals are nonexistent. They are a valuable safety tool in emergencies and can offer peace of mind when exploring off-the-grid destinations.

In conclusion, internet and communication options during RV camping have evolved to meet the needs of modern travelers. Whether you rely on cellular networks, satellite internet, campground Wi-Fi, or a combination of these options, staying connected while on the road has never been easier. The choice of communication method based on your camping style, location, and connectivity requirements. By planning ahead and selecting the right tools and services, you can enjoy a connected and enjoyable RV camping experience while staying in touch with family, friends, and the digital world.

Staying safe while on the road

RV camping offers a unique opportunity to explore the great outdoors with the comfort and convenience of a home on wheels. However, safety should always be a top priority when embarking on an RV adventure. Whether you're a seasoned RV enthusiast or a novice camper, it's essential to take precautions to ensure a secure as well as enjoyable journey on the road.

One of the first steps to staying safe during RV camping is proper trip planning. Make sure you fully understand your destination before you leave, including the route you'll take as well as the campgrounds or RV parks you intend to stay at. Check for road conditions, weather forecasts, and any potential hazards along the way. Be sure to have a well-maintained RV that has been serviced recently to reduce the risk of mechanical breakdowns. When driving your RV, safety starts with responsible and defensive driving. RVs require longer stopping distances to stop because they are heavier and less maneuverable than most other types of vehicles. To stay aware of your surroundings, you should always drive at a safe and reasonable speed, maintain a safe following distance, and frequently check your mirrors. Be mindful of wind and road conditions, as these can affect the stability and control of your RV. If you're new to RV driving, consider taking a safety course to gain confidence and skills.

Seatbelt usage is non-negotiable for everyone in the RV, including passengers. Ensure that all occupants are correctly buckled up while the vehicle is in motion. This applies to both the driver's cabin and any passengers in the living area of the RV. In the event of an accident or sudden stop, seatbelts can significantly reduce the risk of injury.

RV campers should also be aware of the risks associated with carbon monoxide (CO) poisoning. RVs often have gas-powered appliances, such as stoves, heaters, and water heaters, which can produce CO if not adequately ventilated. Always use these appliances according to the manufacturer's instructions, ensure proper ventilation, and install CO detectors inside your RV to provide an early warning if elevated levels of CO are detected.

Fire safety is another critical aspect of RV camping. Equip your RV with smoke detectors, fire extinguishers, and a well-practiced evacuation plan. Never leave cooking appliances unattended, and be cautious when using open flames or portable heaters inside the RV. Make sure you know where the emergency exits are and that they are easily accessible.

Camping in remote or off-the-grid locations can be a thrilling experience, but it also presents additional safety challenges. Ensure you have sufficient supplies, including food, water, and fuel, to last in case of unexpected delays. Be prepared with a first-aid kit and have knowledge of basic first-aid procedures. Additionally, inform someone you trust regarding your travel plans and itinerary, so they can check on your well-being if necessary.

When setting up camp, pay attention to the levelness of your RV and use stabilizers to prevent it from tipping or rocking. Ensure that all utilities, such as electrical connections and propane systems, are properly installed as well as maintained. Be cautious of natural hazards like wildlife, insects, and extreme weather conditions, and take appropriate precautions to avoid encounters or exposure.

Finally, be a considerate and responsible camper by following campground rules and regulations. Respect quiet hours, keep your campsite clean, and properly dispose of trash to minimize the risk of attracting wildlife. Always follow any posted guidelines regarding campfires, pet restrictions, and other campground-specific rules.

In conclusion, staying safe while on the road during RV camping is essential for a memorable and worry-free experience. Proper trip planning, responsible driving, and adhering to safety measures inside and outside your RV are key to safeguarding yourself and your fellow travelers. By taking these precautions and being mindful of potential hazards, you can enjoy the freedom and the adventure of RV camping while ensuring your well-being and peace of mind on the road.

Managing finances and bills

Taking an RV camping trip is a fun way to see the world while having all the conveniences of home on wheels. But handling money and expenses while traveling is an important part that calls for meticulous preparation and arrangement. You can remain in charge of your finances and have a stress-free RV camping experience if you take the appropriate strategy.

Setting up a budget is crucial before anything else for your RV camping trip. As you plan your trip, decide how much you're willing to spend on things like gas, campground fees, food, entertainment, and any unforeseen costs. Setting up a clear budget will make it easier for you to keep track of your expenses and make sure you don't go over your spending limit.

Think about establishing online bill payment and banking services before you leave. You'll be able to pay your bills and handle your finances while on the go with this. You can use your smartphone or tablet to pay bills, transfer money, as well as check account balances due to the mobile apps that most banks and financial institutions offer. Make sure you have all the passwords and login credentials you need to access your accounts from a distance.

It's critical to monitor your spending when you're camping in your RV. Keep a thorough journal of everything you spend each day, including gas, groceries, dining out, campground fees, and other expenses. You can set spending goals, generate financial reports, and keep track of your expenses with the help of a variety of budgeting apps and software.

For recurring expenses like rent or a mortgage, utility bills, and insurance premiums, think about establishing automatic payments. This ensures that essential bills are paid on time, even if you're on the road and may not have easy access to mail or a physical address. Many utility companies and service providers offer online billing and autopay options for added convenience.

Another critical aspect of managing finances during RV camping is to plan for emergencies and unexpected expenses. Create an emergency fund that can cover unforeseen costs like RV repairs, medical expenses, or unexpected travel expenses. Having a financial safety net will offer peace of mind and help you address unexpected financial challenges without derailing your trip.

When it comes to accessing cash, consider opening a bank account with a nationwide or global network of ATMs. This will allow you to withdraw cash without incurring additional fees or surcharges at ATMs located across the country or around the world. It's also a good idea to carry some cash on hand for situations where card payments may not be accepted.

To save money while RV camping, explore cost-effective camping options. Look for campgrounds that give discounts for longer stays or memberships in camping clubs that provide access to discounted rates. Consider boondocking or dry camping, where you camp without hookups in more remote areas, which can be less expensive than traditional campgrounds.

Additionally, be mindful of your energy and water consumption in your RV. Efficient use of resources can help reduce utility costs during your camping trip. Use LED lights, manage your thermostat, and conserve water when showering and doing dishes to minimize expenses.

Lastly, remember to check your mail while RV camping. You can use a mail forwarding service to have your mail forwarded to a selected address or campsite. This ensures that you receive important documents, bills, and mail while on the road, preventing any financial disruptions.

In conclusion, managing finances and bills during RV camping is essential for a smooth and worry-free journey. Establishing a budget, setting up online banking and bill payment services, tracking expenses, and planning for emergencies are key elements of financial management on the road. By taking these steps and being proactive in managing your finances, you can enjoy your RV camping adventure without financial stress and focus on making lasting memories on your journey.

Keeping in touch with loved ones

RV camping offers the freedom to explore new destinations, experience the beauty of nature, and create lasting memories. However, being away from home for an extended period can leave you longing for connections with loved ones. Fortunately, there are several ways to stay in touch with family and friends while on the road, ensuring that you can share your adventures and maintain those important relationships.

One of the most common and convenient ways to keep in touch during RV camping is through modern technology. Most RVs are equipped with cell phone reception and internet connectivity, which makes staying connected easier than ever. Using your smartphone, you can call, text, or video chat with loved ones. Apps like WhatsApp, Skype, FaceTime, and Zoom allow for high-quality video calls, giving you the opportunity to see and talk to family and friends in real-time.

Mobile data plans and Wi-Fi hotspots are also valuable tools for keeping in touch. Based on your location and network coverage, you can access the internet using your smartphone or a dedicated mobile hotspot. This allows you to check emails, browse social media, and send messages. Many RV campgrounds and parks offer Wi-Fi services, making it even more accessible to stay connected.

Social media platforms are another popular way to share your RV camping experiences with loved ones. You can post photos, videos, and updates about your journey on platforms like Facebook, Instagram, and Twitter. This not only keeps your family and friends informed about your adventures but also allows them to feel connected to your travels by following your posts.

For those who prefer a more personal touch, sending postcards or letters is a charming way to keep in touch. While you're exploring new destinations, take the opportunity to pick up postcards or write heartfelt letters to friends and family. Sending these physical tokens of your journey can be a thoughtful and appreciated gesture that bridges the gap between digital communication and tangible connections.

Another option is to schedule regular phone or video call sessions with loved ones. Setting a specific time to catch up can provide a sense of routine and help maintain a strong bond. It also allows you to have uninterrupted conversations and share your experiences in a more meaningful way.

In addition to technological means of communication, consider incorporating your loved ones into your RV camping adventure. Invite family or friends to join you for a portion of your trip or meet up at designated locations along your route. Sharing the experience with loved ones firsthand can create lasting memories and strengthen your connections.

It's essential to maintain a balance between staying connected and fully immersing yourself in the RV camping experience. While it's wonderful to keep in touch with loved ones, remember to also disconnect from technology and savor the beauty of the outdoors. Allocate specific times for communication and set aside the rest of your day for exploring, relaxation, and enjoying the natural world around you.

In conclusion, keeping in touch with your loved ones during RV camping is both achievable and important for maintaining meaningful relationships. Modern technology, including smartphones, internet connectivity, and social media, has made it easier than ever to stay connected on the road. Additionally, personal touches like postcards and scheduled phone calls can further enhance your connections. Balancing communication with the full RV camping experience allows you to create lasting memories while sharing your adventures with those you care about most.

CHAPTER IX

Eco-Friendly RVing

Sustainable RV practices

As RV camping continues to gain popularity, it's essential for travelers to be mindful of the impact their adventures can have on the environment. Sustainable RV practices are becoming increasingly important to reduce the ecological footprint of RV travel and preserve the natural beauty of the landscapes we explore. By adopting eco- friendly habits and making conscious choices, RV enthusiasts can minimize their impact and contribute to a more sustainable way of enjoying the great outdoors.

One of the primary considerations for sustainable RV practices is energy consumption. RVs are equipped with various appliances and systems that require electricity, such as lighting, air conditioning, and refrigeration. To reduce energy usage, consider replacing traditional incandescent bulbs with energy-efficient LED or CFL lights. These bulbs consume significantly less electricity and last longer, reducing the need for replacements. Additionally, make use of natural daylight during the day to minimize the need for artificial lighting.

Proper management of water resources is another critical aspect of sustainability while RV camping. Water conservation is essential, as RVs have limited water storage capacities. Implement water-saving practices like using low-flow faucets and showerheads, fixing any leaks promptly, and reusing graywater (wastewater from sinks as well as showers) for non-potable purposes including flushing toilets or watering plants when permitted.

Furthermore, when it comes to waste disposal, responsible practices are paramount. Dispose of trash and recyclables in assigned containers and follow campground or park rules for waste management. Consider composting organic waste if facilities are available or bringing a portable composting system with you. Also, avoid littering, and pick up any trash or debris you encounter during your travels to leave the natural environment cleaner than you found it.

To minimize your carbon footprint while on the road, prioritize fuel-efficient driving. Maintain your RV's engine and tires for optimal performance, and keep your speed within recommended limits to improve fuel efficiency. Consider using a GPS device or smartphone app that provides information on fuel-efficient routes and nearby gas stations. Reducing unnecessary idling and combining errands can also help save fuel.

Choosing eco-friendly campgrounds and RV parks can make a significant difference in your sustainable RV practices. Look for campgrounds that implement green initiatives, such as recycling programs, energy-efficient facilities, and water-saving measures. Supporting eco-conscious campgrounds encourages environmentally responsible practices within the RV community.

Sustainable food choices also play a role in eco-friendly RV camping. Opt for locally sourced as well as organic foods when shopping for groceries, as they have a lower carbon footprint compared to products that have traveled long distances. Minimize food waste by storing leftovers, planning meals, and composting food scraps when possible. Reducing single-use plastics by using reusable containers and utensils is another way to contribute to sustainability.

Finally, responsible outdoor ethics are essential for preserving the innate beauty of the places you visit. Observe the Leave No Trace guidelines, which include protecting wildlife and other visitors, disposing of waste appropriately, and preserving natural and cultural features. To reduce soil erosion, stick to designated trails. You can also prevent disturbing wildlife by not feeding or watching them from a distance.

In conclusion, adopting sustainable RV practices is essential to minimize the environmental impact of RV camping and protect the natural wonders we cherish. Energy conservation, water management, waste disposal, fuel-efficient driving, and responsible outdoor ethics are all part of a holistic approach to eco-friendly RV travel. By incorporating these practices into your RV adventures, you can enjoy the charm of the outdoors while also leaving a positive and a lasting impact on the environment.

Leave No Trace principles

Leave No Trace (LNT) principles are a set of ethical guidelines established to promote responsible outdoor behavior and minimize the environmental impact of outdoor activities. These principles are particularly relevant to RV camping, where travelers have the opportunity to immerse themselves in nature while also facing the challenge of minimizing their footprint. By adhering to LNT principles during RV camping, travelers can enjoy the beauty of the outdoors while preserving it for future generations.

The initial principle of Leave No Trace is to plan ahead and prepare. This means doing your research before embarking on your RV camping trip. Familiarize yourself with the particular regulations and guidelines of the area you plan to visit. Check for fire restrictions, camping permits, and any specific rules related to waste disposal and campsite selection. Adequate planning also includes ensuring you have enough food, water, and other supplies to minimize your effect on the environment.

The second rule is to camp and travel on sturdy terrain. When RV camping, it's crucial to stick to designated campsites and established roads. Avoid creating new paths or disturbing fragile vegetation by driving off-road or off-trail. Parking and setting up camp on hard, durable surfaces, such as gravel or bare ground, helps protect the natural landscape from unnecessary damage.

Minimizing campfire impact is another critical aspect of Leave No Trace principles. While RVs often come equipped with fireplaces or stoves, it's essential to follow campground rules regarding fires. In areas where fires are permitted, utilize established fire rings or designated fire pans. Keep fires small, use only small sticks and twigs found on the ground, and burn all wood and coals to ash, leaving no trace of your fire behind.

Managing waste properly is the fourth principle of Leave No Trace. RV campers should be diligent in disposing of trash and recyclables in designated containers, both within the RV and at campground facilities. Avoid littering and pick up any trash or debris you come across during your stay. For black and graywater disposal, always follow campground regulations and use appropriate dumping stations to ensure waste is managed safely and responsibly.

The fifth principle is to leave what you find. Avoid picking plants, disturbing wildlife, or removing rocks, fossils, or other natural or cultural features. Preserve the beauty and integrity of the environment by observing it from a respectful distance and appreciating it in its natural state. Leave historical and archaeological sites undisturbed to protect their cultural significance.

The sixth rule of Leave No Trace is to respect wildlife. While it can be exciting to meet wildlife during your RV camping trip, it's essential to watch animals from a distance and avoid feeding them. Feeding wildlife can disrupt their natural behaviors, harm their health, and even create safety hazards for both humans and animals.

Finally, the seventh principle of Leave No Trace is to be considerate of other visitors. Keep noise levels down, especially during quiet hours, to guarantee that everyone can enjoy a peaceful camping experience. Share popular trails and camping areas with other outdoor enthusiasts, and yield the right of way when appropriate. Be mindful of the privacy and solitude of fellow campers, and respect their need for a tranquil outdoor experience.

In conclusion, adhering to Leave No Trace principles during RV camping is not only a responsible and ethical practice but also a way to ensure that the innate beauty of the outdoors remains unspoiled for generations to come. By planning ahead, traveling on durable surfaces, managing waste properly, and respecting the environment, wildlife, and fellow campers, RV enthusiasts can enjoy the wonders of nature while leaving no trace of their presence. Embracing these principles is a commitment to responsible outdoor stewardship and preserving the natural world we cherish.

Reducing your environmental impact

RV camping allows travelers to navigate the great outdoors while also enjoying the comforts of home on wheels. However, it's essential to be mindful of the environmental impact of RV travel and take steps to minimize it. By adopting eco-friendly practices and making conscious choices, RV enthusiasts can reduce their ecological footprint and help protect the innate beauty of the landscapes they visit.

One of the most effective ways to reduce your environmental impact during RV camping is to prioritize energy conservation. RVs come equipped with various appliances and systems that require electricity, such as lighting, air conditioning, and refrigeration. To minimize energy usage, consider replacing traditional incandescent bulbs with energy-efficient LED or CFL lights. These bulbs consume significantly less electricity and last longer, reducing the need for replacements. Additionally, make use of natural daylight during the day to minimize the need for artificial lighting.

Proper management of water resources is another critical aspect of sustainability while RV camping. Water conservation is essential, as RVs have limited water storage capacities. Implement water-saving practices like using low-flow faucets and showerheads, fixing any leaks promptly, and reusing graywater (wastewater from sinks as well as showers) for non-potable purposes including flushing toilets or watering plants when permitted. Furthermore, when it comes to waste disposal, responsible practices are paramount. Dispose of trash and recyclables in assigned containers and follow campground or park rules for waste management. Consider composting organic waste if facilities are available or bringing a portable composting system with you. Also, avoid littering, and pick up any trash or debris you encounter during your travels to leave the natural environment cleaner than you found it.

To minimize your carbon footprint while on the road, prioritize fuel-efficient driving. Maintain your RV's engine and tires for optimal performance, and keep your speed within recommended limits to improve fuel efficiency. Consider using a GPS device or smartphone app that provides information on fuel-efficient routes and nearby gas stations. Reducing unnecessary idling and combining errands can also help save fuel.

Choosing eco-friendly campgrounds and RV parks can make a significant difference in your sustainable RV practices. Look for campgrounds that implement green initiatives, such as recycling programs, energy-efficient facilities, and water-saving measures. Supporting eco-conscious campgrounds encourages environmentally responsible practices within the RV community.

Making eco-friendly food choices is another aspect of RV camping. When grocery shopping, choose organic and locally sourced foods as they have a lower carbon footprint than products that have traveled great distances. Plan your meals, freeze leftovers, and compost food scraps whenever you can to reduce food waste. Another way to support sustainability is to use reusable containers and utensils to minimize the amount of single-use plastics.

Ultimately, maintaining the natural beauty of the areas you visit depends on practicing responsible outdoor ethics. Observe the Leave No Trace guidelines, which include protecting wildlife and other visitors, disposing of waste appropriately, and preserving natural and cultural features. To reduce soil erosion, stick to designated trails. You can also prevent disturbing wildlife by not feeding or watching them from a distance.

In conclusion, adopting sustainable RV practices is essential to minimize the environmental impact of RV camping and protect the natural wonders we cherish. Energy conservation, water management, waste disposal, fuel-efficient driving, and responsible outdoor ethics are all part of a holistic approach to eco-friendly RV travel. By incorporating these practices into your RV adventures, you can enjoy the charm of the outdoors while leaving a positive as well as lasting impact on the environment. Reducing your environmental impact during RV camping is not only a responsible choice but also a way to ensure that the natural world remains pristine for future generations to enjoy.

Contributing to conservation efforts

RV camping offers a special opportunity to connect with nature and explore the great outdoors, and with that opportunity comes a responsibility to help protect and preserve the natural world. Fortunately, there are several ways that RV enthusiasts can contribute to conservation efforts while enjoying their adventures on the road. By taking conscious actions and supporting conservation initiatives, RV campers can make a positive impact on the environment and ensure that these beautiful destinations are available for future generations to enjoy.

One of the most straightforward ways to contribute to conservation efforts during RV camping is to practice responsible camping and outdoor ethics. Familiarize yourself with the Leave No Trace principles, which provide guidelines for minimizing your impact on the environment. These principles include leaving natural as well as cultural features undisturbed, disposing of waste correctly, and respecting wildlife and other visitors. By following these guidelines, you can help protect the delicate ecosystems you encounter while camping.

Choosing eco-friendly campgrounds and RV parks is another way to support conservation efforts. Look for campgrounds that implement sustainable practices, such as recycling programs, energy-efficient facilities, and water-saving measures. By patronizing these environmentally conscious campgrounds, you not only support their initiatives but also send a message to the industry that sustainability matters to RV enthusiasts.

When camping in remote or less developed areas, consider the impact of your camping practices on the environment. Use established campsites and designated fire rings to minimize the impact on vegetation and soil. Avoid creating new paths or disturbing fragile ecosystems. Proper waste disposal, including packing out all trash and following any specific regulations for human waste, is crucial in preserving the innate beauty of the wilderness.

Participating in conservation volunteer programs or initiatives is an excellent way to contribute more directly to environmental protection. Many national parks and conservation organizations offer volunteer opportunities for RV campers to get involved in projects like trail maintenance, habitat restoration, and wildlife monitoring. These experiences not only provide a chance to give back but also allow you to link with like-minded people who share your commitment to conservation.

Another way to contribute to conservation efforts during RV camping is to support organizations and causes that are dedicated to environmental protection. Consider donating to conservation nonprofits, joining organizations like the National Parks Conservation Association or The Nature Conservancy, or purchasing an annual pass that supports national parks and public lands. Your contributions can help fund vital conservation projects and ensure that these natural treasures are preserved for generations to come.

Education and awareness are powerful tools for promoting conservation. Take the time to educate yourself about the ecosystems and wildlife of the areas you visit during your RV camping trips. Talk to other campers and travelers about your passion for conservation and your knowledge of it. Urge others to support conservation efforts by implementing eco-friendly camping techniques.

Finally, think about adopting eco-friendly practices while traveling. Use energy-efficient appliances, LED lighting, and water-saving fixtures to reduce the amount of water and energy your RV uses. Choose sustainable products and reduce single-use plastics by using reusable containers and utensils. By adopting environmentally conscious habits in your RV, you can extend your commitment to conservation beyond your camping trips.

In conclusion, contributing to conservation efforts during RV camping is both a responsibility and an opportunity to make a positive impact on the environment. By practicing responsible camping and outdoor ethics, supporting eco-friendly campgrounds, volunteering for conservation projects, and educating yourself and others about environmental issues, RV campers can help protect as well as preserve the natural world they cherish. Every action, no matter how small, contributes to the greater goal of ensuring that these beautiful destinations are conserved for the enjoyment of future generations. RV camping can be a meaningful way to connect with nature while actively participating in the efforts to protect it.

CHAPTER X

RV Camping Stories

Real-life experiences from RV enthusiasts

RV camping has gained immense popularity over the years, attracting individuals and families seeking adventure, freedom, and a unique way to explore the world. The stories and experiences of RV enthusiasts provide a window into this vibrant and diverse community, showcasing the joys, challenges, and life- changing moments that come with life on the road.

For many RV enthusiasts, the allure of the open road and the freedom to travel at their own pace are the driving forces behind their love for RVing. The ability to wake up in a new location, surrounded by breathtaking landscapes, is a source of constant excitement. Some RV travelers choose to embark on full-time journeys, selling their homes to live a nomadic lifestyle, while others enjoy shorter trips throughout the year. Whether it's a cross-country adventure or it is a weekend getaway, the RV lifestyle offers a sense of liberation and exploration that few other forms of travel can match.

One common thread in the stories of RV enthusiasts is the deep connection to nature and the environment. RV campers often seek out pristine natural settings, national parks, and wilderness areas. The opportunity to camp under starlit skies, wake up to the sounds of nature, and explore remote corners of the country is a source of endless wonder and inspiration. Many RVers share a commitment to responsible camping practices and environmental conservation, understanding the importance of preserving the natural beauty they cherish.

RV travel also fosters a sense of community and camaraderie among enthusiasts. RV campgrounds and parks provide opportunities for socializing with fellow travelers, sharing stories around campfires, and forming lasting friendships. The RVing community is known for its generosity and willingness to help one another, whether it's providing travel tips, lending a hand with RV maintenance, or offering a sense of belonging on the road.

Of course, the RV lifestyle isn't without its challenges, and experienced RVers have their fair share of tales to tell. Mechanical breakdowns, navigating unfamiliar routes, and adapting to life in a confined space can be demanding at times. However, these challenges often lead to personal growth and resilience, as RV enthusiasts learn to problem-solve, adapt, and appreciate the simplicity of life on the road.

One of the most heartwarming aspects of the RV community is the way it accommodates diverse backgrounds, ages, and interests. Families with children share stories of homeschooling on the road, creating lasting bonds, and providing their kids with a unique and experiential education. Retired couples embrace the freedom of RV travel as they explore destinations they've always dreamed of visiting. Solo travelers find empowerment and self-discovery on their journeys, often inspiring others to embark on their adventures.

Real-life experiences from RV enthusiasts also include encounters with local cultures and communities. RV travelers have the flexibility to immerse themselves in the places they visit, trying regional cuisines, participating in local festivals, and learning about the history and traditions of different areas. These interactions not only enrich the travel experience but also foster a deeper appreciation for the diversity of our world.

In conclusion, the stories and experiences of RV enthusiasts reflect a vibrant and diverse community united by a love for adventure, nature, and the freedom to explore. These travelers embrace the challenges and rewards of life on the road, forging connections with the environment, fellow campers, and the cultures they encounter along the way. The RV lifestyle is more than a mode of travel; it's a journey of self-discovery, community, and a celebration of the beauty and diversity of our planet. The real-life experiences of RV enthusiasts inspire others to embark on their own adventures and create their unique stories on the open road.

Memorable encounters and adventures

RV camping is not just a mode of travel; it's a lifestyle that opens doors to unique and unforgettable encounters with nature, people, and the world at large. The stories of RV enthusiasts are filled with remarkable adventures, chance encounters, and experiences that leave lasting impressions, making every journey a tapestry of memories to treasure.

One of the most captivating aspects of RV camping is the opportunity to engage oneself in the beauty of the natural world. RVers often find themselves surrounded by awe-inspiring landscapes, from the majestic mountains of the Rockies to the pristine beaches of the Pacific coast. The moments when they wake up to the gentle rustling of leaves in a dense forest, witness the grandeur of a desert sunset, or fall asleep to the unwinding sounds of ocean waves crashing on the shore become cherished memories that reconnect them with the Earth's wonders.

Wildlife encounters are another source of unforgettable moments in RV camping. While exploring remote and natural areas, RVers often cross paths with diverse species, from majestic elk in national parks to curious raccoons at campgrounds. These encounters offer a sense of connection to the natural world and remind campers of the importance of wildlife conservation. Observing animals in their innate habitats can be both humbling and exhilarating, creating memories that last a lifetime.

The RV lifestyle also provides opportunities for cultural immersion and unique local experiences. RV travelers often seek out destinations that offer a taste of regional culture, cuisine, and traditions. Whether it's savoring authentic Cajun dishes in Louisiana, attending a local powwow in the Southwest, or exploring the history of colonial towns in New England, RV campers can delve deep into the heart of diverse communities and create lasting memories through cultural exchanges.

A hallmark of RV camping is the sense of community and camaraderie among enthusiasts. RVers frequently share stories of campfire gatherings with fellow travelers, where they swap travel tips, trade tales of adventure, and forge meaningful friendships. These connections often lead to joint explorations of nearby attractions, shared meals, and collaborative problem-solving, enhancing the overall experience of RV camping.

Some of the most cherished RV memories stem from serendipitous encounters with fellow travelers. Chance meetings at campgrounds or along the road can lead to lifelong friendships. RVers frequently exchange contact information, promising to meet up again in another part of the country or on a future adventure. These unplanned connections highlight the beauty of human interaction on the open road, as individuals from diverse backgrounds come together to share their love for exploration.

While RV camping is often associated with leisurely journeys and relaxation, it also fosters personal growth and self-discovery. RV travelers often find themselves facing unexpected challenges, from navigating unfamiliar terrain to tackling mechanical issues with their vehicles. Overcoming these obstacles cultivates resilience, adaptability, and problem-solving skills, all of which contribute to personal growth and enrich the journey.

In conclusion, the world of RV camping is a realm of memorable encounters and adventures that inspire a profound appreciation for the beauty of the natural world, the richness of diverse cultures, and the warmth of human connections. The stories and experiences shared by RV enthusiasts reveal the profound impact that this lifestyle has on their lives. These memories of breathtaking landscapes, wildlife encounters, cultural immersion, and meaningful friendships become an integral part of the RV camping experience, shaping the way travelers view the world and their place within it. RV camping is not just a mode of travel; it's a tapestry of moments that create a lifetime of cherished memories.

Lessons learned on the road

RV camping is not just a mode of travel; it's a lifestyle that offers a unique education in self-sufficiency, adaptability, and the art of living in the moment. For those who embrace life on the road, the journey becomes a classroom where valuable lessons are learned, shaping perspectives and imparting wisdom that extends far beyond the confines of the RV.

One of the most profound lessons of RV camping is the importance of minimalism and simplicity. RVers quickly discover that they can live comfortably with fewer possessions and that the true value of life lies in experiences and connections rather than material belongings. The limited space in an RV encourages travelers to prioritize what truly matters, and many find themselves decluttering their lives and letting go of excess baggage.

RV camping also teaches the art of adaptability. Life on the road is unpredictable, with challenges ranging from changing weather conditions to mechanical breakdowns. RVers learn to embrace flexibility, quickly adjusting to unforeseen circumstances and finding solutions to unexpected problems. This flexibility encourages resiliency and inventiveness that are transferable to different facets of life.

An intense respect for the natural world and the significance of environmental stewardship are ingrained in the RV lifestyle. Travelers are constantly surrounded by the beauty of nature, from lush forests to pristine lakes and rugged mountains. This close connection to the environment often leads to a commitment to conservation. RV enthusiasts become advocates for responsible camping practices, practicing Leave No Trace principles and actively supporting efforts to protect and preserve the Earth's natural wonders.

RV camping fosters a sense of wanderlust and a desire to explore new horizons. Travelers learn the art of navigation, honing their map-reading skills and adapting to different terrains and climates. This curiosity and thirst for discovery extend to the exploration of local cultures, traditions, and cuisines. RVers often seek out authentic experiences, immersing themselves in the richness of regional diversity and appreciating the beauty of human connection.

Another invaluable lesson learned on the road is the importance of community and human connections. RV campgrounds and parks serve as gathering places for like-minded individuals, promoting a sense of belonging and camaraderie. Campers share stories, swap travel tips, and forge friendships that transcend geographical boundaries. These connections remind travelers that, no matter where they roam, they are part of a broader community of adventurers.

Patience becomes a virtue in the world of RV camping. Long drives, traffic delays, and the occasional RV maintenance issues all require a patient and calm approach. Travelers learn to embrace the journey itself, finding joy in the process rather than simply focusing on the destination. This mindset shift allows for a deeper appreciation of the landscapes, cultures, and experiences encountered along the way.

Ultimately, perhaps the most profound lesson of RV camping is the realization that life is a journey, and every moment is an opportunity for growth, discovery, and connection. RVers learn to savor the present, cherishing each sunrise, campfire conversation, and starlit night. They understand that the road is not just a means of getting from one place to another but a metaphor for the adventure of life itself.

In conclusion, RV camping is a transformative experience that imparts valuable life lessons to those who embark on the journey. From minimalism and adaptability to environmental stewardship and a deep appreciation for the natural world, the lessons learned on the road are both practical and profound. RVers come to understand that the journey is as important as the destination, and that the true beauty of life lies in the moments of connection, discovery, and exploration. These lessons extend far beyond the RV, shaping the way travelers view the world and the way they live their lives, making the RV camping experience a source of lifelong wisdom and personal growth.

Inspiring stories of transformation

RV camping is not merely a recreational pursuit; it has the power to transform lives in profound and unexpected ways. The stories of individuals and families who have embarked on the RV journey often serve as a testament to the transformative power of life on the road. These inspiring narratives highlight the personal growth, self-discovery, and positive life changes that can occur when one embraces the RV lifestyle.

One of the most common transformations experienced during RV camping is the shift towards a simpler and more minimalist way of living. When travelers step into their RVs, they are confronted with the need to prioritize what truly matters. The limited space encourages them to declutter their lives, parting with unnecessary possessions and attachments. This newfound minimalism fosters a sense of liberation and freedom, as individuals realize that they can thrive with fewer material belongings and that experiences hold far more value than possessions.

The RV lifestyle also encourages adaptability and resilience. Life on the road can be unpredictable, with challenges ranging from adverse weather conditions to unexpected vehicle breakdowns. Travelers quickly learn to embrace flexibility, adjusting to unforeseen circumstances with grace and resourcefulness. These experiences teach valuable life skills that extend beyond RV travel, helping individuals navigate the ups and downs of everyday life with greater ease.

The connection to nature and the environment is another powerful source of transformation for RV campers. Surrounded by the beauty of the natural world, travelers often develop a deep appreciation for the Earth's wonders. They become advocates for responsible camping practices, eagerly engaging in conservation efforts, and actively working to protect and preserve the environment. This newfound commitment to sustainability can lead to lasting changes in lifestyle and consumption choices, fostering a more eco-conscious way of living.

For many, RV camping becomes a catalyst for self-discovery and personal growth. The open road offers a space for introspection and reflection, allowing individuals to gain insights into their values, goals, and priorities. The solitude of RV travel can be a powerful teacher, encouraging travelers to confront their fears, embrace their strengths, and embark on journeys of self- improvement and self-acceptance.

RV camping also nurtures a sense of wanderlust and a desire to explore new horizons. Travelers become adept navigators, honing their map-reading skills and adapting to diverse terrains and climates. This curiosity and thirst for discovery extend to the exploration of local cultures, traditions, and cuisines. RV campers actively seek out authentic experiences, immersing themselves in the richness of regional diversity and fostering a deeper understanding of the world and its people.

Community and human connections are paramount in the RV lifestyle. Campgrounds and RV parks serve as gathering places for like-minded individuals, promoting a sense of belonging and camaraderie. Campers share stories, swap travel tips, and forge friendships that transcend geographical boundaries. These connections become a source of support, inspiration, and personal growth, enriching the lives of RV enthusiasts.

In conclusion, the inspiring stories of transformation during RV camping demonstrate the profound impact that the RV lifestyle can have on individuals and families. From minimalism and adaptability to environmental stewardship and personal growth, the lessons learned and changes experienced on the road extend far beyond the boundaries of the RV itself. RV camping has the power to ignite a sense of purpose, self-discovery, and a deep connection to the world and its wonders. These motivational stories attest to the life-changing possibilities that come with adopting an RV lifestyle and setting out on an epic adventure.

CHAPTER XI

Troubleshooting and Common Challenges

Dealing with breakdowns and emergencies

RV camping offers the allure of adventure and freedom on the open road, but it also comes with its share of difficulties and uncertainties. One of the most daunting experiences for RV enthusiasts is dealing with breakdowns and emergencies while away from the comforts of home. While these situations can be stressful, having a well-prepared plan and the right mindset can make all the difference in making sure a safe and manageable outcome.

First and foremost, it's crucial for RV campers to stay informed and well-prepared before hitting the road. Regular maintenance and thorough inspections of the RV are essential to minimize the risk of breakdowns. Checking the engine, tires, brakes, and all systems before embarking on a trip can help identify potential issues early. Having a basic understanding of the RV's systems and how to perform minor repairs or troubleshooting can also be invaluable.

In case of a breakdown, the first step is to prioritize safety. Pull over to a safe location off the road, turn on hazard lights, and set up reflective triangles or cones to give caution other drivers. Ensure that all occupants, including pets, are safe and away from any potential danger. If it's a mechanical issue, contact roadside assistance or a qualified RV technician for help. Having a reliable roadside assistance plan can provide peace of mind, as it ensures prompt assistance in the event of a breakdown.

Another essential component of preparedness is having the right tools and spare parts on hand. A well-stocked toolbox, including basic hand tools and specialized RV tools, can be a lifesaver in emergency situations. Additionally, carrying spare fuses, belts, hoses, and essential RV repair parts can help resolve minor issues and get back on the road more quickly.

When faced with an emergency, maintaining a calm and collected mindset is crucial. Panic can lead to poor decision-making, while a composed approach can help manage the situation effectively. Communication is key, so ensure that you have a reliable means of communication, such as a cell phone with good coverage, a satellite phone, or a personal locator beacon for remote areas.

Planning for medical emergencies is equally important. Having a well-stocked first-aid kit and knowing basic first-aid procedures can be invaluable in case of injury or illness. It's also essential to familiarize yourself with the locations of nearby medical facilities as well as emergency services along your route. In remote areas, consider carrying a satellite communication device to call for assistance in case of a medical emergency.

Fire safety is a top concern in RVs, given the potential for fires to spread quickly in confined spaces. RV campers should have working smoke detectors and fire extinguishers onboard and ensure that everyone knows their locations and how to use them. Regularly inspect propane systems and appliances, and be cautious when using open flames or portable heaters inside the RV.

In the event of a fire, the immediate priority is to ensure the safety of all occupants. Evacuate the RV as quickly as possible, and call emergency services. If it's safe to do so and you have the appropriate training, attempt to extinguish the fire using a fire extinguisher. However, safety should always come first, and if the fire is spreading rapidly, evacuate and wait for professional assistance.

Weather-related emergencies, such as severe storms or flash floods, can also pose challenges for RV campers. Staying informed about weather conditions and having a weather radio or a reliable smartphone app for weather alerts can provide early warning. In case of extreme weather, seek shelter in a sturdy building or a assigned storm shelter if available. Avoid parking in flood-prone areas and have an emergency evacuation plan in place. In conclusion, dealing with breakdowns and emergencies during RV camping requires a combination of preparedness, calmness under pressure, and the right equipment. RV enthusiasts should prioritize safety, conduct regular maintenance, carry essential tools and spare parts, and have a reliable means of communication and access to emergency services. By being proactive and level-headed, RV campers can navigate unexpected challenges and ensure that their adventures on the road remain safe and enjoyable. While breakdowns and emergencies may be unsettling, they are also opportunities to demonstrate resilience and adaptability, strengthening the bond between travelers and their RVs.

Handling difficult weather conditions

RV camping offers the flexibility to explore various landscapes and regions, but it also means encountering a wide range of weather conditions. From scorching summer heat to torrential rainstorms and freezing winter temperatures, RVers need to be prepared for whatever Mother Nature may throw their way. Handling difficult weather conditions during RV camping requires planning, adaptability, and a focus on safety.

Extreme heat can be challenging for RV campers, especially during the peak of summer. High temperatures can lead to discomfort, dehydration, and potential health risks. It's crucial to have a dependable air conditioning system in your RV to beat the heat. To guarantee that the air conditioner operates effectively, regular maintenance is essential. Additionally, campers should drink plenty of water, avoid physically demanding outdoor activities in the hottest parts of the day, and look for shade whenever they can.

On the opposite end of the spectrum, cold weather presents its own set of challenges. RVs are equipped with heating systems, but they may struggle to keep the interior warm during extremely cold temperatures. To stay comfortable and safe, campers should insulate their RVs, seal any gaps or drafts, and consider using portable space heaters when needed. It's also vital to carry appropriate clothing and cold-weather gear, including winter clothing, insulated sleeping bags, and heated blankets.

Rain can quickly turn an idyllic camping trip into a soggy experience. To handle rainy weather, RV campers should have proper rain gear, including waterproof jackets and boots. Ensure that the RV's roof and windows are sealed and well-maintained to prevent leaks. Have indoor activities or games on hand to keep yourself entertained during extended periods of rain. Planning your trip around the weather forecast can also help you avoid heavy downpours or severe storms.

Snow and ice present particular challenges for RV camping, especially for those venturing into cold climates during winter. Before embarking on such trips, it's advisable to check road and weather conditions, carry snow chains or winter tires if necessary, and be prepared for potential road closures. Insulating the RV and using thermal window coverings can help maintain a comfortable interior temperature. Additionally, having a plan for snow removal from the RV roof is crucial to prevent overloading and potential damage.

Windstorms, while less predictable, can also pose risks to RV campers. Strong winds can affect vehicle stability, create hazards on the road, and even lead to damage. When windy conditions are expected, it's wise to delay travel if possible and seek shelter in a secure location until the winds subside. If you must drive in windy conditions, reduce your speed, use both hands on the steering wheel, and be cautious of wind gusts when passing large vehicles.

In remote or wilderness areas, RV campers may encounter challenging weather conditions like sudden changes in temperature, thunderstorms, or even flash floods. It's essential to stay informed about weather forecasts and local conditions. Carry a weather radio or smartphone app that provides alerts and warnings. Plan your camping locations carefully, avoiding flood-prone areas and areas prone to lightning strikes.

In conclusion, handling difficult weather conditions during RV camping requires a combination of preparedness, adaptability, and a focus on safety. RV campers should be equipped with the necessary gear and clothing for a range of weather scenarios. Regular maintenance of the RV's systems, including heating and cooling, is crucial to ensure they function efficiently. Staying informed about weather forecasts and local conditions is also essential to make informed decisions and avoid potentially hazardous situations. While challenging weather conditions can test the resilience of RV campers, they can also lead to memorable and rewarding experiences if approached with caution and preparation. Remember that safety should always be the top priority when dealing with adverse weather conditions during RV camping.

Addressing common RVing issues

RVing is a beloved pastime that offers the freedom to navigate the world while enjoying the comforts of home on wheels. However, like any form of travel, RVing comes with its own set of challenges and common issues that enthusiasts need to address to ensure a smooth and enjoyable journey. From mechanical problems to navigation mishaps and campsite dilemmas, being prepared and knowing how to handle these issues is essential for a successful RV adventure.

Mechanical issues are perhaps the most common and dreaded concerns for RVers. These can range from engine problems and brake malfunctions to issues with the electrical, plumbing, or HVAC systems. Regular maintenance is the first line of defense against many of these problems. Ensuring that your RV is in top working condition before embarking on a trip is crucial. Additionally, having a basic understanding of RV systems and carrying important tools and spare parts can be invaluable. In the event of a breakdown, having a reliable roadside assistance plan is a lifesaver, as it can provide prompt help and peace of mind.

Navigational challenges are another frequent issue for RV campers. Getting lost or ending up on roads unsuitable for RVs can be frustrating and time-consuming. To address this, invest in a good GPS system specifically designed for RVs, which takes into account the size as well as weight of your vehicle and provides RV-friendly routes. Additionally, always plan your routes in advance, taking into account the height and weight restrictions of bridges and tunnels, as well as the availability of RV-friendly campgrounds along your route.

Finding suitable and available campgrounds can also be a common concern, especially during peak travel seasons. RV enthusiasts should consider making reservations in advance, particularly if they plan to visit popular destinations or campgrounds with limited space. Staying flexible with travel dates and also being open to less crowded or more remote campgrounds can also help address this issue. In some cases, boondocking or dry camping may be a viable option, allowing RVers to camp off-grid in more remote locations.

Propane-related issues can crop up, particularly if you rely on propane for cooking, heating, or powering appliances in your RV. Common problems include running out of propane unexpectedly or experiencing leaks. To address these issues, carry a propane detector to alert you to any leaks and regularly check propane tank levels to avoid running out during a trip. Carrying a spare propane tank can provide a backup source in case of depletion. Additionally, ensure that all propane-powered appliances are in good working order and have them inspected regularly.

Waste disposal and sanitation concerns are common in RVing. Emptying the black and gray water tanks, maintaining proper sewage connections, and preventing odors can be challenges. To address these issues, follow campground rules and regulations regarding waste disposal. Invest in a high-quality sewer hose and fittings to ensure a secure and leak-free connection. Using tank treatments and regularly flushing and cleaning the holding tanks can help prevent odors and maintain sanitation.

Weather-related issues, as mentioned earlier, are also common in RVing. Dealing with extreme temperatures, heavy rain, snow, or wind requires preparation and adaptability. Carrying the appropriate gear, insulating the RV, and monitoring weather forecasts are essential steps.

Being ready to alter travel plans if severe weather is expected is also crucial for safety.

In conclusion, addressing common RVing issues is part of the adventure and can be managed with preparation, knowledge, and a flexible mindset. Regular maintenance, investing in the right tools and equipment, and having a reliable roadside assistance plan are key strategies for dealing with mechanical problems. Proper navigation planning, using RV-specific GPS systems, and being aware of height and weight restrictions can help avoid navigational mishaps. Planning ahead, making reservations, and considering alternative campgrounds can alleviate concerns about finding suitable places to stay. Proactive steps, such as carrying spare propane and conducting regular inspections, can prevent propane-related problems. Maintaining proper waste disposal and sanitation practices, following campground rules, and using tank treatments can mitigate sanitation concerns. Lastly, staying informed about weather conditions and being prepared for various weather scenarios are essential for handling weather-related issues. With the right approach and resources, RVers can navigate these common challenges and continue to enjoy the many rewards of RVing.

Tips for resolving disputes with fellow campers

RV camping offers the perfect opportunity to escape the hustle and bustle of daily life and immerse oneself in the tranquility of nature. However, as enjoyable as it can be, sharing a campsite with fellow RVers can sometimes lead to disputes and conflicts. To ensure a harmonious camping experience for everyone involved, it is essential to be prepared and equipped with strategies for resolving disputes amicably. This section will explore some valuable tips for resolving disputes with fellow campers during RV camping.

First and foremost, effective communication is key when it comes to resolving disputes in any setting, and RV camping is no exception. It's essential to maintain open and respectful communication with your fellow campers. If you have concerns or issues, address them calmly and politely. Engaging in a constructive conversation can frequently lead to a quick resolution, preventing the escalation of conflicts.

Another crucial tip is to be mindful of noise levels and respect quiet hours. Noise disputes are among the most common issues at campgrounds. To avoid these conflicts, familiarize yourself with the campground's specific quiet hours and adhere to them. Keeping noise levels to a minimum during these hours will go a long way in maintaining a peaceful camping atmosphere and preventing disputes with neighbors.

Furthermore, practicing good campground etiquette is essential. Respect your neighbor's personal space and privacy. Avoid encroaching on their campsite, and be mindful of the boundaries. Simple gestures like keeping your pets on a leash and cleaning up after them can also prevent conflicts with fellow campers who may have allergies or simply prefer a pet-free environment.

Additionally, it's important to be considerate when using shared facilities. Campgrounds often have communal areas like bathrooms, showers, and picnic tables. Make sure to clean up after yourself, leaving these areas as you found them. Avoid monopolizing these facilities for extended periods, as it can lead to frustration among fellow campers.

Another tip for conflict resolution in RV camping is to be flexible and willing to compromise. Sometimes, disputes arise due to differences in preferences or expectations. Being open to compromise and seeking mutually beneficial solutions can help resolve conflicts quickly. For instance, if there's a disagreement about the placement of outdoor equipment, consider finding a middle ground that satisfies both parties.

Moreover, it's advisable to be aware of campground rules and regulations. These rules are in place to ensure the safety and enjoyment of all campers. Ignoring or breaking these regulations can lead to disputes and even eviction from the campground. Take the time to familiarize yourself with the campground's guidelines and make sure to follow them.

In conclusion, RV camping can be an incredibly enjoyable and enriching experience, but it's important to be prepared for the possible challenges that may arise when sharing a campsite with fellow campers. Effective communication, respect for quiet hours, practicing good campground etiquette, and being willing to compromise are all essential tips for resolving disputes amicably during RV camping. By following these guidelines, you can ensure a harmonious and enjoyable camping experience for yourself and your fellow campers, allowing everyone to make the most of their outdoor adventures.

CHAPTER XII

After the Adventure

Wrapping up your national park journey

Exploring the beauty and wonder of the national parks is a quintessential American experience. From the majestic landscapes of Yellowstone to the breathtaking vistas of the Grand Canyon, these natural treasures offer a special opportunity to connect with the great outdoors. For many adventurers, RV camping is the perfect way to immerse themselves in the national park experience. In this section, we will discuss the benefits and considerations of wrapping up your national park journey in RV camping.

First and foremost, RV camping provides a convenient and comfortable base for your national park adventures. National parks often offer a range of camping options, but RV camping stands out for its versatility. With an RV, you have a self-contained home on wheels, complete with sleeping quarters, a kitchen, and bathroom facilities. This means you can enjoy the beauty of the national parks while still having the comforts of home, making it an excellent choice for families and those seeking a balance between nature and convenience.

One of the significant advantages of RV camping in national parks is the opportunity to experience the great outdoors at your own pace. Unlike traditional camping, where you might need to set up and break down a campsite each day, RV camping allows you to explore multiple areas within the park without the hassle of constant setup and teardown. You can move from one scenic spot to another, taking in the diverse landscapes and wildlife as you go.

Furthermore, RV camping offers a sense of community that adds to the overall national park experience. Many national park campgrounds have designated RV sites, where you can interact with fellow travelers who share your passion for exploration. Campfire conversations, shared meals, and the exchange of travel tips create a sense of camaraderie among RV campers that enriches the journey and fosters lasting memories.

In addition to the convenience and community, RV camping in national parks allows for a unique connection with nature. Many RV campsites are nestled within or near the heart of the parks, providing you with immediate access to hiking trails, wildlife viewing, and stargazing opportunities. The ability to step outside your RV and be surrounded by the natural beauty of a national park is an experience like no other.

However, it's essential to be mindful of some considerations when RV camping in national parks. First, reservations are often required, especially during peak seasons. National parks are popular destinations, and securing a campsite in advance is crucial to ensure you have a place to stay. Additionally, some parks may have size restrictions for RVs, so it's essential to check the specific regulations of the park you plan to visit.

Another important consideration is environmental responsibility. National parks are pristine and fragile ecosystems, and it's vital to leave no trace of your visit. Follow park guidelines for waste disposal, recycling, and minimizing your impact on the environment. Respect wildlife by watching them from a distance and adhering to park regulations regarding animal encounters.

In conclusion, wrapping up your national park journey in RV camping is a fantastic way to experience the beauty and wonder of these natural treasures. The convenience, comfort, and sense of community that RV camping offers enhance the overall adventure. However, it's crucial to plan ahead, make reservations, and practice responsible camping to ensure that the next generations can continue to enjoy the splendor of our national parks. RV camping allows you to create lasting memories while preserving the natural beauty of these remarkable destinations.

Reflecting on the experience

RV camping is a unique and enriching way to explore the great outdoors, immerse oneself in nature, and create a lasting memories with loved ones. As the sun sets on a campfire-lit evening or you wake up to the sounds of birds chirping in the wilderness, RV camping offers a connection with the natural world that few other experiences can match. In this section, we will reflect on the experience of RV camping, exploring the profound impact it has on individuals and families alike.

One of the most remarkable aspects of RV camping is the sense of freedom it provides. Whether you're navigating the open road or parking your RV amidst the stunning backdrop of a national park, the feeling of liberation from the constraints of everyday life is palpable. RV camping allows you to go wherever the road takes you, whether it's to remote mountain vistas, tranquil lakesides, or pristine beaches. This freedom to choose your own adventure is a significant draw for many enthusiasts.

Moreover, RV camping fosters a deep connection with nature. The RV itself becomes a sanctuary, offering a cozy haven from which to observe the natural world. From the comfort of your mobile home, you can witness breathtaking sunsets, gaze at the star-studded night sky, and listen to the soothing sounds of nature. RV campgrounds often position you in close proximity to hiking trails, wildlife, and scenic landscapes, encouraging exploration and appreciation of the environment.

RV camping is also a social experience that promotes bonding and connection. Whether you're traveling with family, friends, or even meeting fellow RV enthusiasts at a campground, it's an opportunity to strengthen relationships and create cherished memories together. Campfire stories, shared meals, and outdoor adventures forge lasting connections and create a sense of camaraderie among campers.

Another aspect of RV camping worth reflecting on is the simplicity it offers. In a world filled with constant distractions and the demands of modern life, RV camping encourages a return to basics. With limited space and resources, you're prompted to focus on what truly matters. Cooking meals over an open flame, telling stories under the stars, and disconnecting from screens allow for a sense of mindfulness and presence that is increasingly rare in today's fast-paced society.

However, RV camping is not without its challenges. It requires careful planning, from selecting the right RV and campground to preparing for the journey itself. Maintenance and upkeep of the RV can also be demanding, ensuring it remains a reliable and comfortable home on wheels. Additionally, RV camping necessitates adherence to campground rules, environmental responsibility, and respect for fellow campers to maintain a harmonious experience.

In conclusion, reflecting on the experience of RV camping reveals the profound impact it has on individuals and families. The freedom to explore, the connection with nature, the social bonds formed, and the return to simplicity are all aspects that make RV camping a transformative experience. While it may come with challenges, the rewards of RV camping are immeasurable, as it allows us to escape the hustle and the bustle of modern life, rediscover the beauty of the natural world, and make cherished memories that last a lifetime. More than just a trip, RV camping offers us a chance to reestablish relationships with our loved ones, the natural world, and ourselves.

Preparing your RV for storage or the next adventure

Owning an RV provides endless opportunities for adventure and exploration, but it also comes with the responsibility of proper maintenance and preparation. Whether you're stowing your RV away for the winter months or getting ready for the next exciting journey, the way you prepare your vehicle can significantly impact its longevity and your overall experience. In this section, we will discuss the essential steps for preparing your RV for storage or the next adventure.

First and foremost, cleanliness is crucial. Before you tuck your RV away for storage or hit the open road, it's essential to give it a thorough cleaning. Clean the interior to take out any food crumbs, dirt, or moisture that may attract pests during storage. Pay special attention to the kitchen and bathroom areas, as food residue and moisture can lead to mold and odors. On the exterior, wash and wax your RV to protect the paint and the finish from the elements. Cleaning not only helps preserve your RV's appearance but also prevents possible issues down the road.

Another vital step in RV preparation is maintenance. Regular maintenance is the key to keep your RV in top condition and ensuring a safe and trouble-free journey. Check all mechanical systems, including the engine, transmission, and brakes, to ensure they are in working order. Check the tires for any wear as well as tear and make sure they are properly inflated. Check the RV's fluid levels and change the oil and filters if needed. Address any issues promptly to avoid more significant problems later.

For those who plan to store their RV for an extended period, winterization is a critical consideration. Freezing temperatures can cause great damage to your RV's plumbing system, so it's essential to properly winterize it. Drain all water tanks, pipes, and water heaters to prevent freezing and potential bursting. Add antifreeze to the plumbing system to ensure any remaining water is protected. Additionally, consider removing or disconnecting the RV battery and storing it in a climate-controlled environment to avoid damage from cold temperatures.

Interior protection is equally important. To prevent mold, mildew, and odors from developing during storage, consider using moisture-absorbing products like desiccant packets or dehumidifiers. Leave cabinets and drawers open to promote air circulation and minimize the chances of mold growth. Cover your RV's upholstery and mattresses to protect them from dust and moisture. Empty the refrigerator and freezer, leaving the doors ajar to prevent odors.

Properly storing your RV is essential to maintaining its condition. If possible, store your RV under a shelter or cover to protect it from the elements. If outdoor storage is your only option, invest in an RV cover designed to fit your specific model. Storing your RV on a level surface with the tires properly inflated helps prevent uneven tire wear. Be sure to block the wheels to prevent movement.

Finally, if you're preparing your RV for the next adventure, ensure you have all the essentials for a safe and enjoyable trip. Check your kitchen and bathroom supplies, camping gear, and safety equipment. Verify that your RV's registration and insurance are up to date. Plan your route, make campground reservations if necessary, and create a checklist to ensure you don't forget anything important.

In conclusion, preparing your RV for storage or the next adventure is a crucial aspect of RV ownership. Regular maintenance, cleanliness, winterization for storage, and proper storage conditions are all essential considerations. For those gearing up for another adventure, thorough preparation and organization are essential to a smooth and enjoyable trip. By taking these steps, you can ensure that your RV remains in excellent condition and be ready for your next journey or adventure, allowing you to make the most of your RV lifestyle.

The lasting impact of RV camping in national treasures

RV camping is a unique and immersive way to experience the beauty and wonder of our nation's most cherished natural treasures: the national parks. These protected landscapes, from the towering peaks of the Rockies to the sprawling deserts of the Southwest, hold a special place in the hearts of adventurers and nature enthusiasts. RV camping not only provides a means to explore these remarkable destinations but also leaves a lasting impact on individuals and the environment. In this section, we will delve into the profound and lasting impact of RV camping in our national treasures.

First and foremost, RV camping offers an opportunity for individuals and families to forge lasting connections with these awe-inspiring landscapes. The experience of waking up to the sight of towering redwoods, the sound of rushing waterfalls, or the serenity of a pristine lake fosters a deep appreciation for the natural world. This connection goes beyond the immediate thrill of exploration; it instills a sense of stewardship and a commitment to preserving these national treasures for future generations.

Furthermore, RV camping encourages environmental consciousness and responsibility. Campers are more likely to be mindful of their impact on the environment when they are immersed in the natural beauty of the national parks. RV campers often practice Leave No Trace principles, minimizing their footprint, picking up trash, and respecting wildlife and ecosystems. This heightened awareness of environmental issues carries over into everyday life, promoting sustainable practices and conservation efforts beyond the camping trip.

RV camping also promotes a sense of adventure and exploration that can have a lasting impact on one's outlook on life. Venturing into the unknown, whether it's hiking a challenging trail, encountering wildlife, or navigating unfamiliar terrain, fosters a sense of curiosity and a willingness to embrace new experiences. This adventurous spirit cultivated in national parks often extends to other aspects of life, encouraging individuals to step out of their comfort zones and navigate the world around them.

Another lasting impact of RV camping in national treasures is the sense of community it creates. RV campgrounds often bring together people from diverse backgrounds and walks of life who share a common love for the outdoors. Campfire conversations, shared meals, and the exchange of travel stories create a sense of camaraderie among campers. These connections can extend beyond the campground, fostering lifelong friendships and a sense of belonging to a broader community of outdoor enthusiasts.

RV camping also leaves an economic impact on the surrounding communities. National park areas often rely on tourism to support their local economies. RV campers contribute to this by patronizing local businesses, purchasing supplies, and dining at nearby restaurants. This economic support helps sustain the communities that surround our national treasures, ensuring that they can continue to thrive and offer vital services to visitors.

In conclusion, RV camping in our national treasures is not just a vacation; it's an experience that leaves a lasting impact on individuals, the environment, and the communities that surround these remarkable landscapes. The deep connection with nature, the promotion of environmental consciousness, the sense of adventure, and the sense of community all contribute to the transformative power of RV camping. As more and more people embrace the RV lifestyle and explore our national treasures, the enduring legacy of these experiences will continue to shape our appreciation for the natural world and our commitment to its preservation. RV camping is more than a leisure activity; it's a profound and enduring connection to the beauty and majesty of our national parks.

CONCLUSION

In conclusion, "Nomadic Nature: A Comprehensive Guide to RV Camping in National Treasures" is not just a book; it's an invitation to embark on an unforgettable journey into the heart of America's most cherished natural and cultural wonders. Through the pages of this comprehensive guide, readers have been equipped with the knowledge, insights, and inspiration needed to turn their RV camping dreams into a reality.

We've explored the myriad benefits of RV camping, from the freedom of the open road to the deep connection with nature it offers. We've delved into the various types of RVs, helping readers choose the perfect home on wheels for their adventure. We've discussed budget considerations, trip duration, and itinerary planning, ensuring that every aspect of the journey is well-prepared and enjoyable. We've also covered critical topics like selecting the right national parks, understanding reservations and permits, and creating a packing checklist that ensures nothing is left behind.

As the author of "Nomadic Nature," my hope is that this guide has ignited a sense of wonder and wanderlust, encouraging readers to explore the breathtaking landscapes, diverse ecosystems, and rich cultural heritage found within America's national parks. May it serve as a trusted companion on your RV camping odyssey, providing guidance and inspiration as you traverse the open roads, experience the wonders of nature, and make a lasting memories with loved ones. So,

with the road ahead beckoning and "Nomadic Nature" in hand, I invite you to embrace the beauty of RV camping in national treasures. May your journey be filled with discovery, adventure, and a profound connection to the nomadic spirit of nature. Safe travels and happy camping!

Thank you for buying and reading/ listening to our book. If you found this book useful/ helpful please take a few minutes and leave a review on the platform where you purchased our book. Your feedback matters greatly to us.